# HANNIBAL'S ARMY

# HANNIBAL'S ARMY

Ian Stephenson

*Dedicated to*

*My god-children
Catriona and Ross Mayes*

*And to the memory of
My grandparents
George and Margaret Stephenson*

First published 2008
Reprinted 2011

The History Press
The Mill, Brimscombe Port
Stroud, Gloucestershire, GL5 2QG
www.thehistorypress.co.uk

© Ian Stephenson, 2008, 2011

The right of Ian Stephenson to be identified as the Author
of this work has been asserted in accordance with the
Copyrights, Designs and Patents Act 1988.

All rights reserved. No part of this book may be reprinted
or reproduced or utilised in any form or by any electronic,
mechanical or other means, now known or hereafter invented,
including photocopying and recording, or in any information
storage or retrieval system, without the permission in writing
from the Publishers.

British Library Cataloguing in Publication Data.
A catalogue record for this book is available from the British Library.

ISBN 978 0 7524 4121 4

Typesetting and origination by The History Press
Printed in Great Britain

# Contents

List of Illustrations — 7

Preface & Acknowledgements — 11

1. Introduction — 13

2. *Interpretatio romana* — 21

3. Punic Wars — 25

4. Units, nationalities and equipment — 37

5. Hellenisation — 97

Select Bibliography — 117

Index — 119

# List of Illustrations

1 Carthage, as seen from the sea. *Photograph C.M. Daniels*
2 Carthage. Of note, in the centre of the picture are the remains of the circular naval harbour. *Photograph C.M. Daniels*
3 The terracotta elephant figurine from Pompeii
4 A Balearic(?) slinger on Trajan's Column. *Photograph C.M. Daniels*
5 Lead slingshot in the British Museum. These examples are Greek, but are typical of the period
6 A Celtic cavalryman, from Magdalensberg
7 Infantry versus cavalry on the arch at Orange. *Photograph C.M. Daniels*
8 Cavalry combat. On the north relief of the Glanum monument. *Photograph C.M. Daniels*
9 A currency bar, decorated with a Celtic shield, in the British Museum
10 One of the La Tène shields. *Drawn by M. Daniels after Connolly (1978)*
11 A cross-sectional view of a Celtic shield-boss, in the British Museum
12 Celtic shield patterns(?) on the arch at Orange. *Photograph C.M. Daniels*
13 The Vachères warrior
14 Montefortino helmets (in the second row from the top) and their place in the evolution in Celtic helmet design. *Drawn by M. Daniels after Feugère (1994)*
15 The Ciumeşti helmet. *Drawn by M. Daniels after Ritchie & Ritchie (1985)*
16 A Celtic tanged javelin head in the British Museum
17 An Iberian (Spanish) infantryman, armed with a falcata, and protected by a Celtic type shield and a crested sinew helmet
18 An Iberian cavalryman from Cerillo Blanco de Porcuna. Of note is the *pectorale* and the shoulder guards
19 This third-century BC sculpture nicely illustrates not only the *caetra's* layered construction, it also shows both the shield's central grip and its shoulder strap

20  The falcata and its associated dagger. *Drawn by M. Daniels after Quesada Sanz (1997)*
21  The tang of a La Tène period II sword, in the British Museum
22  The sword suspension loop on a La Tène period II sword, in the British Museum
23  The chape from the scabbard of a La Tène period II sword, in the British Museum
24  Two La Tène period II spearheads in the British Museum
25  A Roman Boeotian style cavalry helmet, in the Rijksmuseum van Oudheden in Leiden
26  A Roman example of a Montefortino helmet, in the British Museum
27  A detail of the hinge used to suspend the cheek-piece on a Montefortino helmet, in the British Museum
28  The back of a Montefortino helmet. Note the very small neck guard
29  The simplest form of armour – a trilobate *pectorale*. This example is in the British Museum
30  A Roman Attic helmet, in the British Museum
31  A Roman Etrusco-Corinthian helmet, in the British Museum. This type of helmet, along with the Attic helmet in *31* would originally have been fitted with cheek-pieces
32  *Pila* heads from Telamon. *Drawn by M. Daniels after Sekunda 1996*
33  A third-century BC terracotta statue of a Numidian warrior, from southern Italy
34  Numidian/Mauri cavalry on Trajan's Column. *Photograph C.M. Daniels*
35  The Greek style of cavalry, as depicted on a vase in the British Museum. Of note besides the thrusting spear is the bronze muscled cuirass
36  A Carthaginian cavalryman as depicted on a terracotta plaque from the Douimes district of Carthage
37  A figurine of a Hellenistic period light cavalryman, in the British Museum
38  The Hellenistic Melos helmet, side view
39  The Melos helmet as seen from the front.
40  An early example of what would become the Hellenistic style. This helmet is on the Amazon frieze from the Mausoleum at Halikarnassos in the British Museum
41  The helmet from the Al Sumaa weapons grave. *Drawn by M. Daniels after Horn and Rüger 1979*
42  An Assyrian forerunner of the Al Sumaa helmet, from a relief in the British Museum
43  A muscled cuirass on the fourth century BC tomb of Payava in Xanthos, in the British Museum

*List of Illustrations*

44  A bronze muscled cuirass in the British Museum, note the simple shoulder and side fastenings
45  Protection for the modern rider. This updated version of the muscled cuirass is worn by my god-son Ross Mayes
46  Under-armour padding with *pteruges*, detail from a statue in the Museo della Terme, Rome. *Drawn by M. Daniels after Robinson 1975*
47  A linen(?) cuirass on a funerary relief from Canosa, northern Apulia, now in the British Museum
48  Greek snap-fit bronze greaves in the British Museum
49  An alternative to the *kopis*, the double-edged sword, on a Hellenistic period relief in the British Museum
50  A detail of the hilt of the sword in *49*
51  A *kopis*, as shown on the Amazon frieze from the Mausoleum at Halikarnassos
52  Hoplite warfare, from a relief in the British Museum
53  A hoplite style shield from the Simitthus-Chemtou monument
54  A mail or linen cuirass and Celtic style shield from the Simitthus-Chemtou monument
55  A warrior's panoply – Celtic style oval shield, conical helmet, sword, and spears – on a fragmentary Punic tombstone from D'El-Hofra à Constantine
56  Macedonian phalangite shields. The plain example on the left is from Pergamon, the right-hand shield with the Sun blazon of Macedon is in the J. Paul Getty Museum, Malibu. *Drawn by M. Daniels after Connolly 2000*
57  A reconstruction of a phalangite's shield
58  The *sarissa* and associated finds from Vergina. *Drawn by M. Daniels after Connolly 2000*
59  Reconstructions of the Vergina finds
60  The *sarissa*
61  Reconstructions of Early Modern period pikes. The small heads and tapering shafts of this weapon formed the basis for the latest reconstruction of the *sarissa* in *61 & 62*
62  The pike in action. The weapon is comparable in length to the *sarissa* in *60*

## Colour Plates

1  A Carthaginian war elephant – Second Punic War
2  A Celtic warrior – Second Punic War

3  An Iberian *scutarii* – Second Punic War
4  Italian infantryman/Roman legionary – Second Punic War
5  Numidian cavalryman – Second Punic War
6  Carthaginian cavalryman – Second Punic War
7  Libyan infantryman – Barcid Spain
8  A Hellenistic period helmet from the tomb of Lyson and Kallikles
9  The monument commemorating the Battle of Trasimene
10 Looking towards Lake Trasimene from the monument. Hannibal concealed the bulk of his army in the rolling countryside which rises up from the lake
11 A detail of the Numidian/Mauri cavalry on Trajan's Column. *Photograph C.M. Daniels*
12 A terracotta figurine of a Hellenistic period heavy cavalryman, in the British Museum
13 A La Tène period II iron shield-boss, in the British Museum
14 Reconstructions of third- and second-century BC Roman Republican weapons
15 The carrying system employed on the phalangite's shield
16 The *sarissa* in action

# Preface and Acknowledgements

> For, as I take it, Universal History, the history of what man has accomplished in this world, is at the bottom the History of the Great Men who have worked here.
>
> Thomas Carlyle 1840, 1

The genesis of this work lies some years back in a series of conversations, over coffee, with John Hutcheson, who, sadly, was unable to participate in this endeavour. John was already a Carthaginian enthusiast; I was interested in the subject and had been ever since picking up a copy of Liddell-Harts' *Scipio-Africanus: Greater than Napoleon*. However, more pressing research into other periods had pushed this matter to one side.

Yet the thing would not go away and, slowly over time, I would collect the odd book here, the odd article there, all the while becoming more and more aware that the subject of the Punic Wars as a whole was dominated by, and that Carthage, its inhabitants and army were eclipsed by, the figure of Hannibal. Equally and undoubtedly resultant from this bias, the word Carthaginian tends to raise blank looks until you mention Hannibal. A similar situation exists with Philip II and his far more famous son, Alexander the Great, but that is another matter.

Returning to conversations and coffee, it rapidly became apparent that while a great deal of ink has been spilt on the subject of Hannibal, his 'genius' and which pass he used to cross the Alps, other aspects have been largely glossed over. Of course we assume that this state may have resulted from the paucity of the source material and 'victor's History' is notoriously selective. Alternatively, and returning to the cult of personality, it could be suggested that the success prior to the Punic Wars of the Alexandrian (or should that be Macedonian) art of war has at times tended to be used to gloss over, and not question too closely, the gaps in our knowledge. This book is, as with my earlier works, my attempt at understanding, albeit in this case my understanding having been sharpened by some very enjoyable conversations with John Hutcheson to whom this book is also to some measure dedicated.

Many, many thanks are as ever due to Peter Kemmis Betty and Fiona Mayes. Wendy Logue and Tom Vivian at *The History Press* have to some extent taken the role of Patience on a monument, and for that I am very grateful. In this, as in my previous book, the following also require a mention in dispatches: Lindsay Allason-Jones, Heinrich Härke, Eleanor Betts, Paul Mullis, Alex Croom, Bill Griffith, Ben Andrew, Marcus Daniels, Corin and Nicki Gurr, Jon and Carola Attwater, and, of course, my parents. Susan has gone from driver in the last book to typist in this and thanks are due for her work. Miriam Daniels has, as ever, provided a series of superb illustration.

Finally, my daughter Isabella has as ever been a terror and a distraction, but I would have it no other way.

I.P. Stephenson<br>
Reading, 2007

# 1

# INTRODUCTION

The First World War, the greatest victory the British Army has ever achieved, is probably the most mythologised conflict in British History.
G.D. Sheffield, *The Shadow of the Somme*,
in Addison and Calder (eds) 1997, 29

Certain it is that barely a third part of our army escaped. The annals record no such massacre of a battle except the one at Cannae.
Ammianus Marcellus XXXI.13.18-19

The Punic Wars of 264-146 BC stand as a prime example of Von Clausewitz's dictum that 'war is not merely an act of policy but a true political instrument' (*On War* 1.24). Equally and resulting from this, these very wars, this long century of conflict, occupied a pivotal moment in history, for here we see not the *Kabinettskrieg* of later European history with their limited results – Marlborough, himself, predicted that the War of the Spanish Succession would resolve little and was but the start of a new protracted period of European conflict – on the contrary the conflicts between Carthage and Rome achieved a great deal, for there was a great deal at stake, or at least up for grabs (1).

Whilst it might be tempting to decry inevitability, particularly given the two cities' long, peaceful and to some extent treaty-strewn past, it is equally true that they had definite spheres of influence, and that once all bars and impediments were removed it was inevitable that their spheres would eventually overlap. It is at this point that policy would, of necessity, wield its bluntest of instruments – war.

Inevitability only takes us so far, for whilst there were undoubtedly those in both cities who foresaw the approaching confrontation, the outcome remained

*Hannibal's Army*

*1* Carthage, as seen from the sea. *Photograph C.M. Daniels*

far from certain. For in many ways we are back at the beginning of the Peloponnesian Wars, with two great powers who could no longer peacefully co-exist – detente and cold war were not viable options, yet neither side had the means to rapidly enforce a solution, as each had invested in a different tactical system (*2*). Just as in the earlier conflict between Athens and Sparta, this tactical problem arose in the conflict (the First Punic War) that erupted in 264 BC

*2* Carthage. Of note, in the centre of the picture, are the remains of the circular naval harbour. *Photograph C.M. Daniels*

between Carthage and Rome – how does sea-power defeat land-power, and vice versa?

The First Punic war of 264-241 BC was the longest continuous war in Greek and Roman history. The Peloponnesian war, like the far later Revolutionary and Napoleonic wars of the eighteenth and nineteenth centuries AD was broken mid-course by a temporary peace. However, like the earlier Peloponnesian War, the first war between Rome and Carthage saw a land power become a sea power. For Rome, albeit undoubtedly unconsciously following Sparta, created a fleet and whilst it is true that a number of land engagements did occur, the major clashes of the war took place at sea. The decisive battle of the war was fought off Aegatos Island on the 10 March 241 BC. Ironically it was not Rome's victory, but rather Carthage's action following the peace which so very nearly led to the extinction of the Punic State, with the Mercenary War stretching Carthage to the limit and bringing it closer to the brink of ruin than Rome ever did in over 20 years of continuous conflict.

Into the third century BC, as Lancel observes in his *History of Carthage*, the fates appear to hesitate, unsure in their favour – who would have lordship and dominion, whose Empire would succeed – Rome's or Carthage's? From the dizzying heights of 216 BC it seemed that the balance had tipped in Carthage's favour. The great victory of Cannae and then the defections from Rome, most notably of Capua, had expunged the stains of past ignominy – forgotten was defeat in the First Punic War, forgotten also was the bloody life and death struggle of the Mercenary War and the loss of Sardinia. In its place Carthage was resurgent and triumphant – the new Spanish possessions had not only restored pride, they had filled coffers and created a seemingly invincible war-winning army.

> It might almost be said 'before Alamein we never had a victory, after Alamein we never had a defeat.'
>
> Winston S. Churchill 1951, 354

However, the fates are fickle and 216 BC proved to be the high-tide of Carthaginian success. A lesser state, given the losses in the field and the defection of allies, would have sued for peace – Rome was not such a state. To later generations, as Ammianus testifies, Cannae was a searing event, yet a more defining moment took place in 321 BC at the Battle of Caudine Forks, when the Samnites forced a defeated Roman army to pass under the yoke. This humiliation may go a long way towards explaining the Roman view of warfare and their belief that all struggles were life and death struggles. To Rome defeat was not an option – victory must be pursued relentlessly and at all cost. Rome's towering self-confidence, coupled with massive resources of manpower and steady (and in the case of P. Cornelius Scipio Africanus brilliant) leadership allowed her to not only fight, but win a multi-front war, in the late third century BC. During the Second Punic War Roman armies were fighting in Spain, Sicily, Greece and at sea, as well as in northern and southern Italy. This is not to say that Carthage and her allies meekly collapsed in the face of Roman opposition; there were times when each side experienced the reverse of medal. The final battle of the war, Zama, was fought in Africa in 202 BC. Scipio's defeat of Hannibal, ironically using amongst others the survivors of Cannae, ended the war, while the subsequent peace, although not harsh, effectively ended Carthage as a military power.

Yet it did not spell the end of conflict. Economic resurgence and Roman hubris sounded the death knell of Carthage. The Third Punic War of 149-146 BC saw the fall and sack of the city. As a result of this final defeat a deputation from the Senate:

> … decreed that if anything was still left of Carthage, Scipio [Aemelianus] should raze it to the ground and nobody should be allowed to live there.
>
> Appian, *Roman History*, VIII.XX

As Field Marshal Kitchener asserted in 1915 'we must make wars as we must: not as we would like' and that is equally true of history. From our point of view Rome did the job of destruction too well. Nor has the passage of time helped, for whilst some of the events and protagonists in this drama can (partially) be recaptured in glorious Technicolor, others cannot. Our sources and the physical evidence allow us at times to reconstruct the course of events in the Mercenary and Punic Wars in some detail, yet some aspects remain obscure. For example, despite the gallons of ink spilt on the subject we will in all possibility never be able to correctly reconstruct Hannibal's route from Spain to Italy, particularly his crossing of the Alps – the evidence just does not survive. The current state of our knowledge of the Roman Constitution and Army in this period would, were it not for Polybius and the excursus he penned in Book VI of his *Histories*, undoubtedly be lessened. Indeed so well regarded is his description of the structure and equipment of the Roman Army in the Second and Third Punic Wars that in modern parlance we speak and write of the 'Polybian' legion. However, no equivalent evidence survives for the Carthaginians. Equally, thanks to Plutarch, Polybius, Livy (Titus Livius) and Appian the lives of the Roman protagonists are, in the main, open to us. We will consider the evidence for the Carthaginians, and particularly Hannibal, directly.

Sadly, as has already been said, Rome did its job too well. The fall of the city itself in the third war saw not a Syracusian Solution, simply sacking the city as a prelude to direct Roman rule was not enough. Too much had gone before – Carthage's very existence, its culture, its history, were forfeited by defeat. The destruction of the city to the least and the last (the Roman Senate ordered it razed to the ground and forbade, at that time, anyone to live there) is coupled with the loss, due to vagaries of the passage of time, of works written by Greek and Sicilian historians who were either pro-Carthaginian or who wrote from a Carthaginian standpoint. We thus, as will be seen, face a number of problems in attempting to write an institutional or structural history of the Carthaginian Army, although Hannibal is another matter.

In their histories the Romans lauded him as a great general and a noble enemy, for example Cornelius Nepos, who calls him 'that bravest of men' (*Hannibal* XIII.1). In the cold hard reality of the second century BC, during Rome's rise to dominance of the known world, he was viewed as a threat, possibly even an embarrassment, and as a result his enemies pursued him unto his death. Literary plaudits are all very well and good, but it must be remembered that Nepos, Polybius and the rest were all writing post-mortem, when the threat was in some cases long past. This dichotomy between the unforgiving nature of Roman *real politik* and Roman literary *mores* has, however, allowed Hannibal to slip through the net, to become, to some effect, more than just a name or a vague association with a place, deed, or event, which is the fate of so many of the Carthaginians we come across in our sources.

Today Hannibal is a larger-than-life figure and one of the few figures from ancient history whose name is still known. Mention Carthage to people and you will invariably draw a blank look; the name of Hannibal is, however, immediately recognised (there is also usually some comment made about elephants). Beyond the popular recognition in military historical tomes, Hannibal figures highly in lists and works on the 'Great Commanders' of history. In the ancient works he is ranked alongside Julius Caesar and Alexander of Macedon, and when one considers the whole span of human existence then he is placed with and compared to Robert E. Lee and Napoleon Bonaparte. Whilst it is perenially popular to decry the drawing of such comparisons, it must be remembered that Hannibal himself is also supposed to have engaged in the practice, for according to Livy (35.14) those two old enemies Scipio and Hannibal met in Ephesus, while Scipio was a part of a Roman delegation to Antiochus III, and discussed the greatest generals in history.

Hannibal's fame rests upon his seizure of the strategic initiative and on his three great victories at the beginning of the Second Punic War – of these, although Trebia and Trasimene are still discussed and dissected, Cannae in 216 BC still generates the most interest and not just in historical terms, for General Norman Schwartzkof is reported to have said 'I learned many things from the

Battle of Cannae which I applied to Desert Storm.' As a result both Hannibal and his 'masterpiece' have generated their own body of literature, with Cannae, despite the sterility of the victory, probably being the most discussed of all Roman battles, outstripping more important defeats, particularly the Caudine Forks in 321 BC, the Teutonberg Wald disaster in AD 9 and Adrianopole in AD 378, all of which had a profound impact upon the Roman psyche and policy. However, having said that, while the victory of Cannae was sterile, ironically it was not from the Roman point of view, for it tied Hannibal to a series of alliances in Southern Italy from which he gained little and which limited to some extent his freedom of movement. While Cannae in basic terms simply stiffened Rome's resolve, however, coupled with Hannibal's alliances with those towns and cities which defected to Hannibal, it allowed Rome to bottle up Hannibal in the south of the Italian peninsular and thus gain the strategic initiative. These circumstances, and in particular the cult of personality which has grown up around Hannibal and his victories, coupled with the complete and utter destruction of the Carthaginian state at the end of the Third Punic War, have rather skewed the study of the various protagonists engaged in the Mercenary and Punic wars – with the main loser being the Carthaginian Army.

As with all such studies the evidence divides, in basic terms, into primary and secondary sources, which in turn further sub-divide. The primary sources divide into literary, archaeological and representational evidence, while the secondary split into commentaries on the primary, although along, as will be seen, thematic lines. The main secondary sources pertinent to the Carthaginian army will be treated in this chapter. The primary evidence, its extent and limitations will, however, be examined in the following chapter, *Interpretatio Romana*.

There are of course gaps in our knowledge, but we are still in a position to write a detailed institutional and organisational history of the Roman army in the Republican Period (*colour plate 14*). We can thus talk about the 'Servian' Constitution and the hoplite army; the discussion can then move onto army reform (and the reasons behind it) the rise of the maniple and the structure of the legion. The Polybian Legion can be described, the roles of the tribunes and *legatus* discussed, detailed consideration can be given to the impact of Marius and the Civil Wars on the army etc. etc. (Keppie's 1984 *The making of the Roman Army* remains the best treatment of the subject). The evidence exists to give us a feel not only for the structure of the Roman Army at given times during the Republic, but also allows us to articulate the changes and the reasons behind the changes. The same is not true of the Carthaginian Army. Instead – and this is to some extent apparent from its treatment in the secondary literature – we are left grasping at vignettes.

## Introduction

The main works on the characters, battles and events of the Punic Wars (the Mercenary War is usually slipped in as an aside or interlude in works which discusses all three wars) are also in the main the major secondary works on the Carthaginian Army. Thus we find brief descriptions in, to name some of the works on the subject, Lazenby's *Hannibal's War* (1978) and *The First Punic War* (1996), in Goldsworthy's *Cannae* (2001) and *The Punic Wars* (2000), in Peddie's *Hannibal's War* (1997), in Daly's *Cannae: the Experience of Battle in the Second Punic War* (2002), as well as in Healy's *Cannae 216 BC* (1994), Bath's *Hannibal's Campaigns* (1981) and in Hoyos' *Hannibal's Dynasty* (2003). On top of these and other histories of the wars not listed, the subject of the Carthaginian army usually warrants a chapter or at least an important mention in works on mercenaries, cavalry, elephants and military equipment. For mercenaries see particularly Griffith's seminal *The Mercenaries of the Hellenistic World* (1935) and Yalichev's much more modern *Mercenaries of the Ancient World* (1997). Cavalry is best covered in Gaebel's *Cavalry Operations in the Ancient Greek World* (2002) and McCall's work of the same year entitled *The Cavalry of the Roman Republic*. Elephants, as a subset of cavalry, are well sourced by Scullard in his *The Elephant in the Greek and Roman World* (1974). Although works on the Seleucid and Ptolemaic armies, see particularly those by Sekunda and Bar-Kochva, are also helpful in this and, as will be seen, other areas and in questions relating to the Carthaginian Army. The military equipment of the Carthaginian army is described by Connolly's works *Hannibal and the Enemies of Rome* (1978) and *Greece and Rome at War* (1981), and by Wise's *The Armies of the Carthaginian Wars 265-146 BC* (1992). Polito's *Fulgentibus Armis* (1998) is also valuable, however, the main work on the subject of Carthginian military equipment remains Head's *Armies of the Macedonian and Punic Wars 359 BC to 146 BC* (1982).

Turning to these histories, the problem of describing the structure and organisation of the Carthaginian Army, is described by Lazenby in *The First Punic War* as being 'impossible to say' and this view is to a greater or lesser extent shared by all writers on the subject. For although we are in a position from our sources to list the peoples who fought for and thus made up Carthage's Army – we can list Ligurians, Celts/Gauls, Spaniards/Iberians, Numidians, Greeks, Lybian/African and Balearic Islanders – we hit problems when we attempt to recover command, control and unit structures. Equally tied up with this is the question of who were allies and who were mercenaries. Griffith argues that 'much of the evidence … involved is in a mere splitting of hairs' (1935).

The case for the evidence of the command, control and structure of the Carthaginian army will be considered in Chapters 3 and 4, while the success and failure of the Carthaginian army will be considered throughout the work as a whole, although most weight will be given to the subject in Chapter 3 and 5.

> This is a picture that has always fascinated me. Since I was a child I have wondered why we cannot see those who are carrying the pikes, the people who have done the dirty work of the war. In the game of chess I admire the pawn more than the king, queen, bishops and castles
>
> Arturo Pérez-Reverte, quoted in Moreno 2001, 20

Archaeology is at times considered too much of a blunt instrument to be used in the writing of ancient history, being more concerned and better suited to describing long-term trends than with throwing light on say the actions of or the motives behind an individual or an event. However, archaeology in the form of military equipment studies does allow us to go a long way towards equipping the Carthaginian army. In the process of describing the equipment available to, and thus potentially used by, the various contingents of the Carthaginian army we will (see Chapter 4) edge towards, or at least lay the foundations for, answering some fundamental questions concerning the nature of the Carthaginian army and to some extent illuminating the process of Hellenisation within that army. Thus Chapter 4, as well as looking at unit types and equipment styles, will also survey the evidence for Pérez-Reverte's pikes – what exactly did they look like, how were they carried and, to some extent, used in battle. This chapter will also discuss elephant towers in an attempt to answer the question of whether they were used or not. It will also consider the types of missile troops deployed, although reasons why certain types of troops were favoured over others will be left to Chapter 5.

The last Chapter looks at the military revolution of Philip II of Macedon, at the armies of Alexander's 'Successors' and at the infantry reforms of the 160s BC in order to place the Carthaginian army in context and to gain a feel for the structure of that army in relation to the prevailing military developments of the day.

One final point needs to be made in this introduction and concerns the title of this work as a whole. Although this work is about the Carthaginian army in the First, Second, Third and Mercenary Wars, the nature and extent of the evidence means that this work is primarily concerned with the Carthaginian army of the Second Punic War and more particularly with the army of Cannae and Zama. Thus we will, in the main, be dealing with and describing Hannibal's Army.

# 2

# INTERPRETATIO ROMANA

Reports that say something hasn't happened are always interesting to me, because as we know, there are known knowns; there are things we know we know. We also know there are known unknowns; that is to say we know there are some things we do not know. But there are also unknown unknowns – the ones we don't know.

Donald Rumsfeld, U.S. Secretary of Defence 2001-2006

David Starkey, in a lecture on Henry VIII, describes the Tudor Period as the ideal period to study. Now such a claim may be dismissed as being purely a subjective observation based, given the fact that he (Starkey) is primarily an historian of the English Court, upon the towering personalities who bestrode the political stage in this country between AD 1485 and AD 1603. Equally, of course, it could be argued by any student of the 'great man' school of history that their period was ideal for similar reasons. However, Starkey's argument was actually empirical in nature and was in fact based upon the quantity of the evidence available. There was, he declared, a sufficiency of information on the Tudors, i.e. there is a lot of evidence, but not so much as to make it impossible for one person to study and be familiar with it. After the Tudor period there is an ever increasing surfeit of evidence, but before this period we have, the further back one goes, an ever decreasing supply. Thus the Tudors are the prefect period to study. Of course one can debate the specifics of this argument, and in the Ancient World the Romans stand out as an evidence high point. The Carthaginians, however, do not stand out; indeed they rather confirm the general thrust of Starkey's argument.

Carthage at the time of its destruction was older than Rome, having been founded in the ninth century BC by Phoenician traders from Tyre. Throughout its history it maintains its links, predominately via trade, with the Eastern Mediterranean, while its location and maritime nature also opened up the Western Mediterranean to its ships, its merchants, and its influence. It was a well ordered, civilised polity and when thinking of Carthage and its fate one is reminded also of the Incas and Aztecs. History is written by the victors, yet we know from the writing of the winners that in antiquity at least the writings probably of the losers, but definitely of those more sympathetic to the losers, did exist – and thus we begin to approach the heart of the problem. For the situation with Carthage is like Rumsfeld's now infamous quote and it is also like Albrecht Dürer's rhino.

Dürer never saw a rhinoceros, rather his AD 1515 drawing of the creature is based on another's sketch as well on a description of the animal in a letter he received from Lisbon. We are in a similar position to Dürer in that any attempt to reconstruct Carthage is in the main based upon the observations of outsiders, not unfortunately on the views of the inhabitants themselves.

Defeat in the Second Punic War marked the end of Carthage as a power, defeat in the Third marked the end of if it as a civilisation. The total destruction of a civilisation is an uncommon event and in this case we should not look back with wistful nostalgia – Carthage played and lost – except possibly in relation to primary evidence, of which we should regret the loss. With the Roman Army we are to a large extent spoilt by the seemingly endless wealth of primary evidence – but even here we still have gaps. Carthage on the other hand is very much at the other end of the primary evidence spectrum. As a result, and in order to attempt to reconstruct the Carthaginian army, we do at times have to cast our net rather wide.

The phrase *Interpretatio romana* is generally translated as the 'Roman Interpretation', although it could also mean, as Kulikowski argues, the Roman distortion or filter (depending of course upon your point of view). It is generally used by scholars in relation to Rome's barbarian enemies, for to the Greeks and Romans barbarians were barbarians and if they needed to be categorised, by the likes of Tacitus in his *Germania*, then they were slotted into a series of existing criteria and so classified. Now this is not to say that the Carthaginians were barbarians, but we are faced with the fact that our surviving main primary literary sources for the three Punic Wars are Romano-centric. Of course in the writing of a politico-military history of the events of the Punic Wars this is not really a problem, and any good history of the wars, such as those by Lazenby or Goldsworthy, will nicely take you through the pitfalls, whilst still providing a cogent narrative, even though at times we are reliant upon a single source. In, for example, the particular instance of the Third Punic War we have to use Appian, who although not as good a historian as either Polybius or Livy, is all we have and to reject him in favour of nothing would be churlish. Nor does the problem lie in a lack of objective criticism of Rome and its actions, or with praise for Hannibal and his successors – all of which we find in our sources. No, the problem from the point of view of studies such as this lies in the fact that whereas Polybius (to take the best example) provides a detailed description of the Roman Army (hence we are able to talk about the Polybian Legion) he does not appear to have extended the same courtesy to Carthage. Now Polybius was primarily concerned with explaining the primacy of Rome to a non-Roman audience – thus discourses, such as those on the Roman's political and military systems are pertinent and relevant to the aim of his work. Equally, surviving copies of Polybius, and for that matter Livy, are incomplete. We thus enter the realm of what they may have contained. In the same sphere reside the known, but now lost, pro-Carthaginian works, particularly the works of Sosylos and Silenos, Greek historians – the former from Sparta, the latter from Kaleakte in Spain – who accompanied Hannibal and wrote histories of the war. While the First Punic War from a Carthaginian standpoint was described in the third century by the Sicilian historian Philinus, that too is now lost. Surviving works and fragments do, of course, contain information on the Carthaginian Army, how could they not? Yet this was not their primary concern, far from it. Their concern was Rome – therefore although we are in a position to glean some information concerning the organisation and equipment of the Carthaginian armies of the Punic Wars, our state of knowledge in relation to these matters is less than that for the Roman Army of the same period.

Our other main source of information, archaeology, is, as mentioned, a blunt instrument better suited to trends than to specific events. Kalkriese (the site of one of the major events in the AD 9 Teutonberg Wald disaster) stands as an exception, and although one can always find exceptions, it equally remains true that in the main this discipline remains better suited to discerning and defining long-term trends. As with the loss of the literature, the destruction of the city in the middle of the second century BC has, in archaeological terms, served us ill. True, a number of Carthaginian and Numidian finds including monuments and reliefs do exist, but the amount of evidence is not great. Purely military finds – reliefs etc. – particularly once the naval evidence is removed, generally amount to a series of either single finds or a handful of similar items. Thus we have evidence for helmets, armour, shields, spears and javelins, and a sword, but not enough if we are reliant solely on the North African evidence to provide anything near to a coherent picture. We are actually better off as we will see, in archaeological terms, when we turn to look at the equipment of those groups who, as mercenaries or allies, fought for the Carthaginians, such as Spaniards, Celtiberians, Celts and others. However, as with the Roman Army of the Republic we flounder when we come to reconstruct the clothing and personal equipment of the Punic army. The archaeological and representational evidence on these subjects is poor in the extreme.

In order to counter these difficulties we do at times have to cast a wide net. Such casting is generally in the direction of the Eastern Mediterranean and the heart of the Hellenistic World. This is because it is likely, given Carthage's known connections with the Greek world, that although not a full part of the mainstream of the Greco-Hellenistic world, they would have taken on board and copied many aspects of that world (this argument is considered and developed more fully in the final chapter of this work). The Hellenistic world, its military culture and importantly the greater amount of evidence (archaeological, literary and representational) which exists for it, thus provides a parallel upon which we can, to some extent, build our model of the Carthaginian army.

We thus have at times an apparently disparate evidence base. Furthermore, we have to remember that at times we are filtering what evidence we have through Romano-centric sources and contemporaneous Hellenistic parallels. Yet for all of that we are still able to paint, if not a complete picture, then at least a picture of the Carthaginian army at the time of the Punic Wars.

# 3

# THE PUNIC WARS

> A Victory is the greatest tragedy in the World except a defeat
> The Duke of Wellington, 1815,
> quoted in Howarth 1980, 27

The sun, rising over the field of Cannae on the morning of 3 August 216 BC looked down on a scene no less than death, an image of hell drawn from Bosch or Dante made real. For there, crammed into a horribly small space, lay the dead of one of the most complete slaughters of any age. Fifty thousand Romans, more than twice the number of British dead from the first day of the Somme, the majority of the double consular army which had marched out of its camps on the previous day to such high hopes, lay dead upon the field. They were destroyed, according to some estimates, at a rate of 200 men per minute, by a numerically inferior force led by Carthage's greatest tactician – Hannibal. For Hannibal it was the zenith of his career. For Rome? Well for Rome it, along with defeats at Lake Trasimene and at Trebia in the preceding years, goes a long way towards explaining Marcus Porcius Cato's second century BC demand – '*Delenda est Carthago*' – Carthage must be destroyed (Plutarch, *Cato the Elder*, 27).

It is all too easy when one looks at the events of the early years of the Second Punic War to ascribe everything to Hannibal. Yet was this the case? Where did the impetus for the war and the strategic direction of it come from? Were tactical decisions the purview of the general himself or were they decided in council? Finally, how original was, and indeed ultimately how successful were these decisions in what we might call the great scheme of things (always remembering of course that Hannibal and Carthage in the end lost the war).

Nature abhors a vacuum – the same is equally true of politics. The disappearance of Pyrrhus from the Romano-Punic geo-political world allowed for an expansion in the future belligerent's spheres of influence. Cold War is a product of the Nuclear Age – the inability to launch a wholly successful first strike, coupled with the doctrine of M.A.D. or Mutually Assured Destruction, ensured that there was and is more to gain from peace and absolutely everything to lose in war – thus there is peace between the superpowers. However, prior to M.A.D. and the Nuclear Age, war was an inevitable consequence of the rivalry between powers.

Von Clausewitz, in his great treatise *On War*, observed that 'war never breaks out wholly unexpectedly' (1.7). Beevor, commenting on the fact that historians, understandably, shy away from not only the word but the very concept of inevitability, goes on to argue that the fact remains that at times, and Spain in the late 1930s is one such case, it seems impossible to envisage a set of circumstances that would not have led to the events that subsequently transpired – in Spain's case, civil war. The same is true of the conflicts between Rome and Carthage.

The problem was Sicily. War would have in all probability eventually erupted between Carthage and Rome, but Sicily certainly precipitated it. The island was too strategically important to be allowed to be dominated by a potentially hostile power, for control of Sicily, even hegemonic control, facilitated the projection of power and influence across the Mediterranean. In this light Rome's decision to send troops across the Straits of Messina, and thus precipitate the First Punic War, is not, and at the time probably was not, such a big step as later commentators make out.

The First Punic War began in 264 BC, and from then until its conclusion in 241 BC the majority of the campaign took place either in Sicily or in the seas around it, with the decisive battles of the war taking place at sea. However, in 256 BC in an attempt to end the war, the consuls L. Manlius Vulso and M. Atilius Regulus defeated the Carthaginian navy off Ecnomus on the southern coast of Sicily before proceeding to invade Africa. Vulso did not remain in Africa, having been ordered home. Regulus, with some 15,000 foot and 500 horse advanced on Carthage. Defeating a Punic force at Adys, he then seized Tunis. Tunis now appears to have acted as Regulus' base from which he devastated the surrounding countryside causing the surrounding towns to surrender to the Romans in scores. The two sides now entered into negotiations to end the war; a force of less than 16,000 men had humbled the might of Carthage and left it staring defeat in the face. Things were black, but they were not quite that black. Regulus proved to be an astute strategist, but an arrogant negotiator and the talks dragged on, giving the Carthaginians time to set their military affairs in order. Carthage, following the fashion of the day, used mercenaries and had been recruiting in Greece since the beginning of the war, and at this crucial juncture help arrived. Not in the form of a great body of men, but in the person of the mercenary general Xanthippus. We will look in greater detail at Xanthippus later in this chapter, however, he was able to reorganise the Carthaginian army and lead it to victory over Regulus' Roman force. Regulus was captured, subsequently dying in captivity, possibly by torture. The defeat of Regulus ended all hopes for an early conclusion to the conflict. Africa was not invaded again, although it was raided. The war dragged on inconclusively in Sicily, and at sea, with neither side committing either the resolve or the resources to achieve victory. Finally, in 243 BC the Romans prepared a new, and hopefully war-winning fleet. The final decisive battle of the war was fought of Aegates Island on the 10 March 241 BC. The subsequent Roman victory and its consequent naval supremacy forced the Carthaginians to the negotiating table and peace on Rome's terms. Rome's victory saw it rise to become the premier power in the Western Mediterranean and also placed Sicily firmly within Rome's sphere of influence.

Carthage's cup of sorrow was not yet full, although it must be said that the next disaster which befell the Punic state was entirely of its own making. Carthage was in many ways a more Greco-Hellenistic state than Rome, and thus it hired mercenaries, both specialist individuals such as Xanthippus, and bodies of troops. Rome, victorious in what would become the First Punic War, required Carthage to remove its troops from Sicily. The repatriation of the native Carthaginian forces to North Africa was not a difficulty, but a problem arose with the 20,000 mercenaries who had fought for them. Initially shipped back in small groups, they then camped together and demanded their back-pay. Carthage refused. As a result of this refusal the mercenaries marched on Carthage and, copying Regulus, they camped at Tunis. Again as with Regulus, Carthage began to concede. Negotiations then got out of hand. The mercenaries became greedy and factions within the mercenary force, fearful for their future, caused the negotiations to fail. They seized and killed the Carthaginian negotiators thus provoking war. The Mercenary War of 240-237 BC saw the Libyans attempt to shake off Punic hegemony by joining the mercenaries – the non-inclusive nature of the Carthaginian state was reaping its rewards. The war of 240-237 BC, like all similar civil conflicts, was noted for its ferocity and cruelty, for it saw Carthage's own citizens take up arms against their sister cities of Hippou and Utica, as well as against some of her own Libyan and Numidian subjects and allies. The war ended with Carthage victorious, but during its course Rome had heaped a further indignity on its former enemy. In 238 BC at the urging of Carthage's Sardinian mercenaries, who were also in revolt against their employer, Rome annexed Sardinia.

The year 237 BC saw Carthage emerge from the trauma of the Mercenary War impoverished and humiliated. A fleet, gathered to regain Sardinia, had been warned off by Rome. Hamilcar Barca (Hannibal's father) the commander of the fleet, had done well in Sicily during the First Punic War, was the most successful Carthaginian general of the Mercenary War and now turned his sights on Spain.

Trade, and its concomitant small-scale settlement had long linked Carthage to Spain. Hamilcar, who is reported to have virulently hated the Romans, saw Spain as a means of regaining Carthage's pride as well as filling her depleted coffers. It did both. Hamilcar died in 298 BC while extending Carthage's Spanish empire. He was succeeded by his son-in-law Hasdrubal, who continued his father-in-law's policy of, at times aggressive, expansion.

It was likely that whosoever lost the First Punic War would, at some later date, seek to reverse the decision of that first conflict. Rome's victory elevated it to the position of the premier power in the Western Mediterranean. From this position Rome kept a wary eye on its defeated neighbour. Thus Rome dispatched an embassy to Hasdrubal, leading to the subsequent Ebro Accord of 225 BC, which was, from Rome's point of view, simply an exercise in power and control. Rome would allow Carthaginian expansion, but within limits and provided it did not threaten Rome or her interests. The Ebro river was simply a line in the sand, beyond which Carthage could not go, although one must wonder (and indeed doubt) that it had any real meaning to Rome, other than as an exercise in super-power politics.

Hasdrubal was assassinated in 221 BC. Carthaginian-controlled Spain now passed into the hands of Hasdrubal's brother-in-law, and Hamilcar's eldest son, Hannibal. Like his father, Hannibal is supposed to have had a passionate hatred of Rome. He also saw himself in a position to fully realise his father's dream. Spain had not only refilled the Carthaginian treasury, it had also provided her with a manpower reserve. The only thing wanting for Carthage's pride to be fully restored was a defeated Rome. Regulus' invasion of North Africa had almost ended the first war – was it possible to do the same, bring Rome to her knees by an invasion of Italy? Hannibal evidently thought that it was. How though to accomplish it? The quickest route was by sea but Roman naval supremacy ruled this out, for any invasion fleet, with ships packed with soldiers, was too vulnerable to enemy naval action. If the Romans caught Hannibal's army at sea the invasion would be over before it began and Carthage's pride would once again be drowned in the waters of the Mediterranean. Thus Hannibal's, now famous, march across the Alps.

The Second Punic War opened well for Carthage. Hannibal successfully led his army from Spain, crossed the Pyrenees and then the Alps, before leading his army into plains of northern Italy, where he gained his first great victory over the Romans, in December 218 BC, at the River Trebia near Placentia. He repeated his success the following year, 217 BC at Lake Trasimene in Etruria. 216 BC saw him in Apulia, in south-eastern Italy. Here at Cannae he achieved his greatest victory. For Rome, 216 BC and the debacle of Cannae was the nadir of their fortunes. For Hannibal the successes of the previous three years were delusory. Rome refused to capitulate, and the diplomatic successes resultant from Cannae – a number of towns and cities repudiated their alliance to Rome and came over to Hannibal, plus Philip V of Macedon entered the war on Carthage's side – brought little or no real aid to the Punic cause. Instead Rome, marshalling its vast well of manpower, proceeded to learn from the mistakes of the past. Bottling up Hannibal in southern Italy and avoiding direct battlefield confrontations with him, it went on to win the war in Italy by slowly clawing back its lost Italian territory. Hannibal's new allies were too scattered for him to be everywhere at once, they thus fell one at a time. Outside of Italy, Roman armies checked Philip in Greece and even the revolt of Syracuse in 214 BC came to nought. After a great siege, and despite direct Carthaginian assistant, Syracuse was taken and sacked by Marcellus in 212 BC. Rome also directly intervened in Spain, but the first Roman force to land there in the year of Trebia, 218 BC, although initially successful, was defeated and its commanders killed in battle in 211 BC. It appeared as if the Roman adventure in Spain was over. However, the Carthaginians failed to utterly destroy the Roman force, and although driven to the edge of the sea, it was still there when P. Cornelius Scipio, son and nephew of the army's dead commanders, arrived to take charge in 210 BC. The younger Scipio's subsequent brilliant campaigns from 210-206 BC ended Carthaginian rule and saw the beginnings of Spain's history as a province of Rome. Returning to Rome, and the consulship in 205 BC, he took Sicily as his province. The island was to be the springboard for the Roman invasion of Africa. Scipio landed in Africa in 204 BC and the following year, 203 BC, saw his victory at Great Plains. Carthage panicked and recalled its remaining forces, principally Hannibal's, from Italy. As with Regulus, Carthage was negotiating with Rome with one hand, whilst seeking a military solution with the other. The return of Hannibal and his army precipitated the last battle of the war. In 202 BC at Zama, somewhere near Carthage (the exact site of the battle is unknown) Hannibal, and thus the Carthaginian state, were defeated at the hands of a Roman army led by P. Cornelius Scipio, who was subsequently entitled *Africanus*

Defeat in the first war saw merely a downgrading in Carthage's status, defeat in the second saw her cease to be a military power; moreover as a result of treaty obligations she was practically made subservient to Rome particularly in the field of foreign affairs. The Third Punic War of 149-146 BC stemmed from the fact that just over a half century after her defeat Carthage was once again resurgent, albeit largely in financial and trading terms. For Rome this was simply too much to bear, and according to Appian, the Roman senate sought a pretext for war. The Treaty of 201 which ended the Second Punic War forbade Carthage to make war in Africa without Rome's permission. They had, however, ignored this in 151-150 BC, when albeit unsuccessfully they had raised an army and gone to war against their Numidian 'neighbours'. This treaty violation gave Rome the pretext it needed, not for declaring war, but for the heaping of more and more unreasonable demands on the Carthaginians. The upshot could only be war, the outcome of which could never really be in doubt, despite initial Roman incompetence. The Third Punic War was fought entirely in Africa, and rapidly developed into the siege of Carthage. The reason it lasted so long was that the city possessed formidable defences and the performance of the Roman army was poor at best. The situation changed with the appointment as consul, in 147 BC, of P. Cornelius Scipio Aemilianus, the son of Aemilius Paulus, who had been adopted into the great Africanus' family. Bringing energy and professionalism to the Roman war effort, he successfully concluded the siege in 146 BC. For the Romans the problem of Carthage could not be solved by treaties and payments – Carthage, as Cato said, 'must be destroyed', and so it was. The conclusion of the Third Punic War saw the Romans raze the city of Carthage to the ground and forbid further settlement on the site. The Carthaginian state ceased to exist.

Our understanding of the Punic Wars is essentially Roman and as a result we are, particularly for the second war, in a better position to examine the strategic direction of the war from a Roman standpoint. In Rome the *cursus honorum* (the career pattern for Roman senators in the Republic which consisted of alternating increasingly senior civilian administrative and military posts) irrevocably intertwined civilian and military life – here civic militarism reached if not its apogee then certainly one of its finest flowerings. Carthage on the other hand kept these two strands of society separate – certainly military success was a route to civic power, but it does not appear to have been the only route. Thus, whereas the Roman system of yearly commands firmly delineated strategic direction within the Roman Senate, in Carthage the appointment of generals to accomplish a specific task, without timescale, to some extent placed the complete strategic direction of a war with the commanding general, and gave at times a greater freedom of movement that was permitted under the Roman system.

Carthaginian generals could not of course escape civilian oversight, but as with the Barcids in Spain and later in Italy, as Hoyos argues, his family's political domination of their home city, which came about as a result of Hamilcar's successes in the Mercenary War, allowed Hannibal not only complete freedom of movement, but also to some extent allowed him to attempt, if not control then at least direction, of the other spheres of the conflict. However, whereas the Roman Senate kept a very firm, and it must be admitted a remarkably successful, hand on the tiller, the same cannot be said for Carthage and Hannibal. Nowhere is this better seen than in Spain against the younger Scipio, where rivalries between the commanding Carthaginian generals and either the lack of, or the inability of, an overall commander in the province, allowed Carthage's forces to be defeated in detail. Indeed this lack of a strategic overview, which is something we will return to when assessing Hannibal's generalship, materially contributed to Carthage's failure in the Second Punic War.

Command above the level of the phalanx, unit or warband, appears with a few exceptions to have been reserved for Carthaginian citizens. Indeed what we can tell from the history of the city as a whole is that over time the citizen body became more concerned with trade and commercial success, the fruits of which allowed for the hiring of troops, which further lessened the appetite of the majority for military service. This was not true of everyone, or rather it was not true of what could be called the officer class. Nor, one suspects, would Carthage have wanted it so, for it is generally safest to have the command of troops in the hands of those who have a vested interest in the state. On top of this, and we are best informed regarding Hannibal and his staff, we see family and political connections playing an important part. This is most obviously the case in Carthaginian, or as some have argued, Barcid Spain, where the original commanding general Hamilcar Barca was succeeded by his son-in-law Hasdrubal, who was in turn succeeded on his death by his brother-in-law Hannibal Barca. Equally when Hannibal set out for Italy he left behind one brother, (another) Hasdrubal, to command in Spain and took with him his other brother, Mago, to whom he entrusted the ambush at Trebia. The commander of the Numidian cavalry at Cannae, Hanno son of Bomilcar, appears to have been a nephew, while the commander of the Celtic and Spanish cavalry at the same battle, yet another Hasdrubal, appears to be unrelated, but was undoubtedly politically connected to the Barcid party. Alongside these we also know of a Carthalo, a Gisgo and most famously Maharbal, who Plutarch labels Barca.

In 215 BC Hannibal, taking thought as to the future direction of the war, particularly given Rome's failure to capitulate after Cannae, signed a treaty with Philip V of Macedon. Any hopes of seeing Macedonians fighting alongside Hannibal's forces in Italy were soon dashed as Rome, aware of the negotiations, sent troops to Greece to contain the Macedonian threat. Important in this context, however, are the names of three Carthaginian senators, Mago, Myrcan, and Barmocar, whose names are associated with the treaty and appear to have acted as civilian advisors to the commanding general – Hannibal in this case – but we should expect to see similar groups attached to Carthage's armies in Spain.

These men, these officers and senators, were aristocrats to a man and together formed the army's military council. Hoyos postulates that representatives from the army's national contingents may have been present – if so then they were there probably solely as observers. Equally, given that they were all under senior

Carthaginian officers, then it is possible that they were not even present at all. On top of this the military council may have been purely advisory and when Hannibal was riding high, probably no more than a 'rubber-stamp' body – Polybius (3.85.6) states that Hannibal consulted and tested his ideas on his brother Mago and his friends. It may be then that it was an inner-circle, not just in Hannibal's own force, but in all Carthaginian armies, of trusted friends and family, who truly advised and helped the commanding general to reach and make the real decisions. In this context the full military council would only meet once a decision had been reached, to hear what was planned and to receive their orders.

Before finally going on to examine Hannibal's record, we will first consider the exceptions to the Carthaginian stranglehold on the senior command positions. As we have already stated it does of course make sense to have Carthaginian officers commanding not simply the army as a whole, but also the main constituent groups of said army. Equally in such a diverse force, in terms of the various national and ethnic groupings present within the various armies of the Punic state, in Italy, Spain, and North Africa, we should expect to find individual units commanded by their own native chiefs, lords and warleaders (as we shall see in the next chapter). We do, however, occasionally have evidence for some non-Carthaginians commanding larger bodies of troops. The most interesting example (Livy 25.40.5) is one Muttines, a Libyan-Phoenician. Trained by Hannibal he went to Sicily in 212 BC to command the Numidian cavalry there. The interest lies in the fact that he points to the possibility that our limited knowledge might be slightly misleading us and that the high command structure within the individual Carthaginian armies might not have been as uniformly dominated by the city's citizens as the rest of the evidence leads us to believe. More famous of course is the case of Xanthippus in the First Punic War. Xanthippus' rise to army command was, however, more a product of the situation than of any openness in the Carthaginian military structure. Regulus' invasion of North Africa had placed Carthage not simply in a perilous state, but had brought it to the verge of capitulation. Yet as the Greek mercenary general Xanthippus (one hopes tactfully) pointed out to his new employers, Carthage had all of the right pieces on the board, it was just not moving them correctly. Xanthippus' subsequent professionalisation of Carthage's land forces and his consequent victory over the Romans has been frequently retold and it is not necessary to do so again. What is important to consider is his departure. As an encouragement to others, Carthage crucified generals who failed. The whole thing is very reminiscent of the Athenian attitude to perceived military failure, with the 'scapegoating after Arginusae' (to quote Hanson) being the most obvious example springing to mind. The system, like all such systems, was of course subject to political interference. Now Xanthippus had not of course failed, quite the opposite in fact, thus crucifixion was not at that moment in the picture. However, the crucial bit is *at that moment* – for leaving aside Polybius' more fanciful story (36.4), as he more plausibly asserts (36.2-3), Xanthippus undoubtedly departed in order to avoid the jealousy which was likely, and we can speculate that at the back of his mind he viewed the price of failure as much too high, more so because, as an outsider he would have had little if any political support. Thus Xanthippus, although interesting, is most probably atypical.

> Then said Maharbal 'In very truth the gods bestow not on the same man all their gifts; you know how to gain a victory, Hannibal: you know not how to use one.'
>
> Livy, XXII.LI.4

> Even if the French were to lose a battle on their own territory, it would never cause them to conclude peace; rather their patriotism would cause them to summon up all the strength of their resource-rich land.
>
> Helmuth Graf von Moltke (the Elder), quoted in Foley 2005, 18-19

We do not know if Maharbal ever uttered these words or if they are purely an invention of Livy's. No matter what the truth, they do, I believe, provide the best assessment of Hannibal's character. Equally von Moltke would I think have understood the Romans better than Hannibal. Hannibal is one of the few generals, in fact one of the few people from ancient history whose name is still widely known today. He is nowadays lauded and studied as a military genius. His name is romanticised and he has joined the pantheon of great losers, standing alongside the likes of Napoleon and Robert E. Lee. Even over this stretch of time he is the glamorous, plucky underdog – but in many ways he is glamorous in that his name casts a glamour or delusive spell.

Hannibal's genius rests upon his overland invasion of Italy, his three great victories, and his subsequent long campaign in Italy. Taking his three great victories first – the Battles of Trebia, Trasimene and Cannae show that Maharbal was right, Hannibal did know how to win battles (*colour plates 9 & 10*). However, in tactical terms we see nothing innovative. The double envelopment as a tactic goes back to the Battle of Marathon in 490 BC and was certainly attempted, albeit at sea, during the First Punic War, while the ambush which the Carthaginians pulled off so successfully at Trebia was very much a common-place of Greco-Hellenistic warfare and from his education we know that Hannibal was well versed in that world. True, the bowing of his centre at Cannae was innovative, but it was a gamble, for at his two previous encounters the superior Roman infantry had punched through his line. At Trebia and Trasimene this had simply led to escape, rather than anything more serious. In the early years of the Second Punic Wars Hannibal was lucky in his opponents, which in itself is not something to be taken lightly.

However, equally Hannibal did not understand his adversaries. The war, which he had by his actions started, was predicated upon victory in the field leading to political capitulation. Certainly three major defeats in as many years and a butcher's bill of some 80-85,000 dead, would have led any other Hellenistic state to seek terms. Rome was not any other Hellenistic state – instead Rome was like the France described by von Moltke. Yes some towns and cities did desert Rome after Cannae, but they did not provide Hannibal with either a massive manpower boost, a major port, or more crucially a 'domino effect'. Many of the defectors were more simply anti-Roman, rather than positively pro-Hannibal. As for the years after Cannae and before Zama, yes he maintained his army in what was effectively enemy territory, but to what purpose? His failure to take a major port, combined with his native city's fear of the Roman navy, meant that aid from home was negligible. His brother Hasdrubal, who followed in his footsteps, was decisively defeated before he could achieve a union with his brother's army. The Roman's did obligingly throw Hasdrubal's head at a Punic outpost – it was thus brought from there to Hannibal. The revolt in Syracuse, the death of the elder Scipio in Spain and the treaty with Macedon were all strategic opportunities which came to nought. Yes, Rome was forced to keep troops in Italy in order to bottle up Hannibal, but that did not stop them at the same time waging and winning a multi-front war. After the political failure of Cannae, Hannibal became a tactical nuisance (albeit one who did not stop Rome from taking back her lost territory) and a strategic irrelevance.

Going back slightly (in some ways to go forward) Lazenby in his apology for and defence of Hannibal after Zama, argues that in Scipio's invasion of North Africa we are seeing but a pale copy of the brilliantly innovative march from Spain. Yet if anyone was being, to use Lazenby's own words, obvious and pedestrian, it was Hannibal. Two previous invasions of North Africa, by Regulus and even earlier by Agathocles the Tyrant of Syracuse, both almost ended in Carthage's defeat. The potential success of taking the war to the enemy's very gates was thus there for Hannibal to see in even a very cursory study of his city's own history.

Finally to the Battle of Zama. The battle itself took place in 202 BC, near Carthage, although the exact site remains unknown. Hannibal fielded a force of some 40-50,000 men, drawn up in three lines, with approximately 80 elephants stationed in front of the first line of the Carthaginian forces. Facing them, under Scipio, were 23,000 foot again drawn up in three lines and 5500 horse. The battle opened with cavalry skirmishes on the flanks. Hannibal then ordered in his elephants. Scipio had, however, foreseen this and not only were there lanes between the Roman maniples down which the elephants were funnelled, but he also ordered all of the army's trumpets to blow which disorientated some of the beasts driving them back onto their own cavalry. The elephants had singly failed to shatter the Roman lines. At this point the Roman cavalry charged their already confused opponents, driving them off the field and pursing them. Both sides were reduced to blocks of infantry, although the Carthaginians had the numerical advantage. Hannibal, eschewing manoeuvre, attacked head on. The Roman infantry, however, proved superior in close hard fighting. The Romans crushed Hannibal's first two lines, comprised of mercenaries, and Carthaginians and Libyans respectively. Hannibal's third line was made up of his Italian veterans, who were fresh having as yet taken no part in the battle; they are also believed to have equalled in numbers Scipio's infantry. Having crushed the first two lines Scipio halted, calmly redressed and redeployed his forces. Keeping the *hastati* in the centre and moving the *principes* and *triarii* to the flanks he extended his line so that it now overlapped the Carthaginian line and thus negated Hannibal's numerical superiority. Redeployment in the face of the enemy is one of the hardest manoeuvres to successfully execute and this was the ideal time for Hannibal's veterans to attack the Roman infantry. The chance was missed. Hannibal watched the manoeuvre and then waited for the Roman advance to resume. A hard fought infantry engagement ensued. Yet for all that Hannibal's veterans were fresh, they failed to make any headway against the Romans. The issue was decided by the return of the Roman cavalry. Falling on the back of the Carthaginian third line, which was now assailed from two sides, they cause the line to break. Hannibal lost approximately half his force at Zama, some 20,000 men. The death toll was lower than Cannae, but the result was more decisive. The Second Punic War was over. Carthage had lost.

Like Napoleon at Waterloo, excuses are advanced for Hannibal's failure to win. The gods forbid that there was actually someone around better than him and that he was simply out-generalled, and by a mere Roman at that! In the end I think the best verdict on Hannibal may be taken from Wellington's comment at Waterloo about his more famous, more glamourous and less talented opponent:

> Damn the fellow, he is a mere pounder after all!

# 4

# Units, Nationalities and Equipment

> Hannibal crossed the river at break of day, after sending ahead of him the Baliares and the other light-armed troops, and posting each corps in line of battle, in the order in which he had brought it over.
>
> Livy XXXII.XLVI.1-2

We are here predominantly concerned with the army Hannibal led into battle at Trebia, Trasimene, Cannae and ultimately Zama. The Barcids in Spain will also be considered, as will to a lesser extent the forces of the Mercenary War, as well as the First and Third Punic wars. However, as in all matters involving the Carthaginians, we are constrained and must therefore in the main deal with Hannibal.

This chapter is very much a 'naming of parts'. The question is, however, how do we go about naming them? Units or troop types are to a large degree defined by their organisation and equipment. Yet in the case of the Carthaginians we are probably best supplied with information concerning their equipment and from that we can infer other things. Before moving on to the questions of equipment, we must first discuss army organisation in terms of unit types, size and nationality, but not to any great extent command and control, for we have already covered that aspect of Punic warfare in the previous chapter.

When speaking, in military terms, of organisation it is customary to divide armies, primarily, into their basic parts – infantry, cavalry and even though we are in the ancient world, one can still speak of artillery. Further subdividing would then occur – infantry and cavalry would be divided into light and heavy, and again because this is the ancient world we would include elephants as a sub-type of cavalry (*colour plate 12*). Certainly if we were writing about the Roman Army of the Punic Wars that is how we would do it. Indeed, staying with Rome for a moment, we would then go on to discuss the legion as described in detail by

Polybius, with an examination of legionary structure considering the three lines of heavy infantry (the *hastati*, *principes* and *triarii*) along with the cavalry and *velites* (skirmishers). We would then be in a position to talk about, discuss and describe the maniple system and the centurionate. We would also (and in fact we will) talk about the *socii* or allies.

The Carthaginian Army, however, permits none of this. In fact in some respects when we use the phrase Carthaginian army we are to some extent perpetrating a misnomer and we will deal with this problem before returning to our organisational problems, although the two are to some extent connected.

The Carthaginians had armies, as did the Romans and the Anglo-Saxons – to argue otherwise would be faintly ridiculous – and yet we cannot talk about the Carthaginians in the same way as we would talk about the other two. True the Carthaginians employed (in the loosest sense of the words) all of the basic ingredients we would expect – heavy and light infantry, heavy and light cavalry (including elephants) as well as artillery/siege equipment – but for all of this an important difference remains.

The army of the late Anglo-Saxon state, the army of Maldon, Fulford and Hastings, was to all intents and purposes a larger version of the armies of the English Conquest. The warriors of an individual lord in the fifth century AD had grown by the eleventh century into the army (basically a collection of warbands) of a king. This was equally true of the Romans. The regular army created by Octavian, like all other aspects of the Augustan settlement, has its roots in the Republic and thus the force created in the first century BC, which lasted up to the late third century AD and the reforms of Diocletian, would have been recognisable to and understood by Marcellus and P. Cornelius Scipio in the third century BC and Polybius in the second century BC. For with both the Anglo-Saxons and the Romans we see continuity of structure, recruitment and organisation over time – in fact over centuries. We are thus able to talk of typical standard armies.

Carthaginian armies were at times all the same and yet all different. The sameness came from their common structure, while the diversity derived from the various contingents which made up the armies. We have already covered command and strategic direction (or the lack of it) in the previous chapter. Here we are looking at contingents and equipment. The unique nature of every Punic army derived from the fact that although they were all commanded and led by Carthaginian citizens, no two armies were alike in their composition, as they were made up of a variety of groups/nationalities whose allegiance was not always necessarily to Carthage. Thus we see bodies of troops or units raised from subjects and allies, as well as mercenaries, and including the occasional unit of Carthaginian citizen troops. This is why, given the sheer diversity of

## Units, Nationalities and Equipment

nationalities that were potentially present, we cannot speak of a typical army and why, particularly when it comes to the equipment, we will consider it in terms of ethnic or national group as opposed to a more conventional troop type breakdown. Thus in the First Punic War we see Libyans, Spaniard and Balearic Islanders, Numidians, Ligurians, Celts and Greeks, as well as Sardinians and Corsicans. While in the Second or Hannibalic War we have Libyans, Liby-Phoenicians, Numidians, Spaniards and Balearic Islanders, Celtiberians and Celts, Ligurians and, after Cannae at least, Italians. Thus we see both differences and similarities in the range of peoples who fought for the Carthaginians, as well as some obvious overlaps between the two main wars.

For those contingents and, particularly for the period of the Second Punic War, we are in a position to discuss their equipment (even if at times it is in the most general of terms). What is harder and what we have problems with is their organisation – how big were they? How were they commanded at a unit level? Did they exist as sub-units? Equally their method of recruitment remains speculative – were they allies or mercenaries? Or were they subjects supplied by treaty?

Before turning to the subject of equipment we will first consider unit size, composition, and recruitment. However, it must be noted that, as with all things Carthaginian, the evidence is less than perfect. Polybius (1.33.6 and 15.12.7) describes both Xanthippus' army and Hannibal's in 255 BC and 202 BC respectively as phalanxes, while he says that the Spaniards and Celts at Cannae were deployed in *speirai* (Polybius 3.114.4). Despite this apparent precision we have a problem. The problem of interpretation lies with the impression given by the language in this context, at best, as one will see, the words merely serve to give an impression of size.

In Macdeonian terms, specifically during Alexander's invasion of Asia, a (the) phalanx comprised 9000 men. The smallest sub-unit was the file (16 men under the command of a *lochagos*) with the main tactical unit being the *taxies* (1500 men under the command of a *strategos* or *taxies*). However, Polybius (15.12.7) also uses the word phalanx to describe Roman *hastati*, again specifically at the Battle of Zama. Scipio had some 23,000 infantry at Zama of whom, and Lazenby is most probably correct that we cannot put an exact figure on the breakdown of Roman infantry in the battle, some 6500 were *hastati*. We are thus looking, in Carthaginian terms, at a unit of between 1500 and 9000 men. However, Polybius uses the word to describe the whole of Hannibal's final line, which is believed to have equalled in numbers the whole of the Roman infantry in the final phase of the battle. Thus in reality all we are seeing is Polybius using the word to describe a large body of close-order infantry. Given that we do not have exact figures for the size of the Carthaginian army at Zama, any attempt to apply exactness to a word which can have such a general meaning is doomed to failure. We of course experience a similar problem when we examine the use of the word *speirai*. As with phalanx, Polybius also uses the word *speirai* in a Roman context. At Polybius 6.24.5 & 8 he uses the word to describe maniples. In Roman terms a maniple, the word originally meaning handful, was a tactical sub-unit and consisted of either 120 *hastati*, the same number of *principes*, or 60 *triarii*. In the non-Roman context of the Spaniards and Celts who formed a part of Hannibal's army of Italy, we are probably best advised to return to the original meaning of the word maniple – namely a handful. The wars of this period were conducted by soldiers and warriors. The Romans, the Macedonians and Libyans fall into the former category, whereas the Celts, Celtiberians, Spaniards and Numidians belong in the latter. Here we would define the difference as one of organisation – an army of soldiers was heavily organised, in terms of a set unit and command structure. Soldiers would be paid, uniformly equipped, heavily drilled and trained. Soldiers are not individuals, rather they are a part of a whole. Warriors, conversely were individualistic, the ties that bound them were concerned with prestige, reputation and kinship. Equally with warriors we see little emphasis on drill or uniformity.

The Spaniards, Celts and Celtiberians were warriors – they did not fight in nice, ordered maniples, their formation was the warband. The question 'how big was a warband?' is of course without a definite answer, being dependent upon the now unknown variations of the level of prestige and the amount of territory controlled by the chieftain or warleader. However, Polybius' equation of the warbands with the maniple suggests that such formations numbered 100-200 men. Daly puts an upper limit of 500, which is possibly a bit high, but all figures in this area are mere supposition. At best we can say that the size of individual warbands numbered men in the low hundreds and certainly not in the thousands. As for the other contingents who made up the Punic armies, and especially that of Hannibal, some we have a degree of information on, but with others we can merely speculate. The Ligurians, like their Celtic neighbours and allies, were in all probability organised as warbands, as indeed were the Celtiberians and the Lusitanians. For the Balearian slingers we can give the numbers deployed at various times in the Second Punic War – for example in 218 Hannibal dispatched 870 to Africa and retained 500 in Spain (Polybius III.33.5-16), yet beyond instances such as this we cannot really advance our organisational understanding. With those Italians who defected to Hannibal after Cannae we should expect them as for all Roman *socii* or allies to be organised along Roman lines. The Numidians operated in tribal groups thus, like the Celts, Iberians and the other similar contingents in Carthage's service, we should expect to find units comprised of several hundred men per unit. However, Livy (25.17.3 and 27.26.8) also potentially gives us an insight into the makeup of the Numidian cavalry, for he does at times refer to them as operating in squadrons, or as he puts it *turmae* – the Roman military term for a force of some 30-36 men. Now it is unlikely that Numidians were quite as precisely divided as a regiment of *Ala*, rather what we are seeing is a small tribal sub-unit based upon family and kinship groupings. Livy merely chose a word known to himself and his audience to describe, in a military context, a small group of horsemen who formed a part of a larger whole. Yet the principle is the same – the family groups (or *turmae*) came together to form the tribal force (continuing the analogy – the *ala*).

As we saw in the last chapter, high command was, with a few notable exceptions, the preserve of the Carthaginian citizen elite. It is believed that Xanthippus, as a part of his professionalisation of the Carthaginian military, introduced or as Daly puts it 'remodelled' the Punic command structure along Spartan lines.

> When a [Spartan] King is leading the army, all orders are given by him. He himself gives the necessary instructions to the polemarchs and it is passed on from them to the regimental commanders, from them to their company commanders, from them to the platoon commanders, and from them to their platoons.
>
> Thucydides, *History of the Peloponnesian War*, 5.66

Of course similar command structures existed in those other great professional armies of the ancient world, the Roman and Macedonian armies. However, given the apparent failures in the Carthaginian army of the mid-third century BC and given the fact that Xanthippus was either a Spartan or Spartan trained, then it seems likely that whatever system of command existed prior to his employment was replaced or remodelled using the Spartan system as a template. It is equally likely that as the Carthaginians and Libyans fought as close-order infantry, based upon the hoplite model, that any pre-existing system was similar to the Spartan system, albeit not as tight or as strictly enforced, and that the existing base made it easier to impose and implement Xanthippus' new system. Of course the Spartan hierarchy of command (*Polemarchs, Lochagoi, Pentecontores, Enomotarchs*) applied only to the soldiers and not to the warriors in Hannibal's army – the Libyans and, at Zama, the Carthaginians. The Carthaginians by the time of the Second Punic War provided an officer class, but save when their city was directly threatened, as was the case during Scipio's invasion of Africa at the end of the Second Punic War, Carthaginian citizens did not fight *en mass*. This changes again in the Third Punic War, when of necessity Carthage's citizens fought to defend their city from the Roman besiegers. Those other soldiers, the Italians (former *socii* or allies of Rome) were organised along Roman lines and the basic contingent from each town was the *cohors* or cohort – roughly 500 men strong – plus one or more *turmae* of cavalry commanded by a *praefectus*. Each cohort contained maniples of *hastati*, *principes* and *triarii* thus allowing it to fit seamlessly alongside the legions order of battle.

Soldiers enjoy layers of command, warriors do not. Warbands were built on the personality and commanding presence of their leader. As a result the stratigraphy of command with its associated levels of officer, which we see in more civilised armies, was not compatible with the warband structure. Rather the chief or warleader could issue his commands and orders to the groups as a whole. True there would be trusted lieutenants within the warband, usually the leader's own kinsmen, who could be trusted at times to lead sections, but such cases lacked the formality of the junior officers, the platoon leaders that we see in the Spartan Army. Equally, where you have an army comprised of warbands then the chain of commanders was very short and direct. The king (effectively a chief of chiefs) issued his orders to the leaders of the various warbands and they in turn issued them to all of the men they commanded. As for the Numidian squadrons we have already encountered (again see for example Livy 25.17.3) it is impossible to say whether or not they constituted individual warbands or if they represented parts of a warband on detached service under the command of a trusted subordinate.

After Hannibal, the elephant is probably the most famous part of the Carthaginian Army. In the year 228 BC, at the time of the death of Hannibal's father Hamilcar and of the accession to high command of Hasdrubal, his brother-in-law, the Carthaginian elephant corps in Spain stood, according to Diodorus, at 200, one of the largest of the period. By 218 BC and the beginning of the Second Punic War it appeared to have reduced in size to a mere 58 elephants – 21 of whom remained in Spain under Hannibal's brother. The remaining 37 entered history and embarked upon the invasion of Italy. How though were such forces organised and commanded? I. Maccabees (6.30) gives the Seleucids 32 elephants 'trained for war', while at Magnesia Livy (XXXVII.40) has the elephants, again Selecuid, deployed on the flanks in groups (or herds) of 16, as well as in pairs between the divisions of the phalanx. In the work the *Outline of Tactics by Asclepiodotus the Philosopher,* chapter IX is concerned with elephants, their organisation and command structure. In it, Asclepiodotus, takes the basic sub-unit to be two elephants, building up in multiples (2, 4, 8) to 16 – 16 elephants formed an *elephantarchia* – after which we see large formations being made up of multiples of 16. This neat picture of sub-units and units based upon multiples of two and particularly 16 fits nicely with Livy and I.Maccabees. However, once we move beyond this we must either sacrifice neatness or postulate under- and/or over-strength units, if of course we accept the universality of Asclepiodotus' model. For at Raphia in 217 BC the Seleucid King Antiochus deployed 102 elephants, 60 on the right wing and 42 on the left, whilst earlier against the rebel Molon he used a mere 10 elephants. While, as we have seen, the Barcids in Spain had at one time a massive force of 200, only 37 were used to invade Italy and at Zama the Carthaginians again deployed, to little effect, some 80 elephants. Asclepiodotus was writing an ideal, although it is likely that at least some of his command structure, particularly the rank of *elephantarchia* (commander of the elephant corps) was used even in the Carthaginian army. Is impossible to say how closely his other sub-divisions were followed.

Hanson in his paean to citizen militias, *Why the West Has Won*, rightly stresses the supremacy of civic militarism. Yet the Carthaginians abandoned this form, using their trading wealth to pursue other avenues. Carthaginian armies are commonly referred to, usually in derogatory terms (they did lose after all) as mercenary armies. However, the mercenary status of their armed forces is not quite so clear-cut as it may first appear, nor was the use of such troops out of step with the thinking of the day. Mercenaries are professional soldiers who are hired to serve a foreign power for payment and the war which immediately followed the First Punic War and which brought Carthage to the edge of ruin is rightly called the Mercenary War. Carthage's failure to treat the large number of mercenaries who had fought for it against Rome adequately, precipitated the conflict. However, whilst the evidence for the hiring of troops in the First Punic War is relatively straightforward, it must be conceded that the evidence for the Second Punic War is not so clear cut.

Griffith (1935) views the whole matter as 'a mere splitting of hairs', given the contemporary contradictory language. Rome at the beginning of the Second Punic War could, according to Polybius, draw upon a manpower reserve of 700,000 citizens and allies. This massive well of men liable for military service put the Roman state in an enviable position and it is with this in mind that we should view Livy's depreciating remarks concerning Carthage and it resources. Three factors caused the increase in the use of mercenaries in the fourth and third centuries BC. The first factor was the Peloponnesian War, which created a supply of men trained for war; the second the increasing professionalism as typified by the Macedonian army; finally there was the money. In the case of Macedon and the 'Successor states', the wealth of the conquered funded vast military expenditures. In the case of Carthage, vast wealth founded upon trade allowed them to import hired help to stand against Rome's militaristic society. Yet the question of who was hired, who were levies and who were allies is not quite so straightforward as our sources would have us believe. There is of course an exception to this ambiguity and that is the case of the Balearic slingers. They appear without question to have been mercenaries. For the rest, as will be seen, they constituted a mixture of allies, subject levies and mercenaries, although uncertainty exists as to the degree of each.

Despite the fact that the Carthaginians ruled large parts of Spain and North Africa we cannot simply view these troops as either allies (in the Roman sense) or as subject levies. The problem, as with most problems concerning the Carthaginian army, lies in the language and the vagaries of the surviving sources. For it is not simply a case of saying that they were paid – where then does one draw the line between mercenaries and loyal citizen soldiers? Equally Appian in his work *The Punic Wars* (XII.80) tells us that Carthage surrendered 'complete armour for 200,000 men', many times more than would be required to arm any force of citizens, thus implying that the Carthaginian state supplied and equipped those Africans who fought for them. Such a situation would put the Libyans into the category of subject levies, since mercenaries supplied their own arms and armour. Complicating, or rather confusing the issue, we have Polybius, who refers to the Libyans as mercenaries in the First Punic and Mercenary Wars, yet in the Second Punic War he is not so specific, save at the Battle of Zama when he places them in the second line of infantry, deliberately setting them apart from the mercenaries who formed the first line. Livy fails to clarify the issue. Livy was a product of his age, a true Augustan, and the same can be said of his monumental history. As MacDonald, in *The Oxford Classical Dictionary* (1970, 615), puts it:

> He [Livy] set himself to give Rome a history that in conception and style should be worthy of her imperial rise and greatness.

In this context Rome's triumph in the Second Punic War was in Livy's eyes nothing less than the triumph of the Roman system. In simple terms (and why from Livy's position of hindsight complicate the matter?) it was the triumph of the citizen soldier over the mercenary.

It is of course too simplistic to simply state that the Carthaginian army was purely composed of mercenaries and yet the evidence, such as it is, does not allow us to construct a terribly nuanced picture, rather we can reach general conclusions. Carthage ruled or held hegemony over large tracts of Spain and North Africa, and as such was in a position to command subject levies. However, the prominent part played against the city by its Libyan subjects during the Mercenary War may well have influenced Carthaginian attitudes towards its future conquests in Spain and for the subsequent war with Rome. Thus Carthage may have gone from raising subject levies to hiring and equipping volunteers, allies or subject contingents, we cannot be sure of their exact relationships. For example, the Numidians provided troops as allies and even though Carthage was the senior partner in the alliance and exercised overall command and control, it remained the case that the Numidians required wooing. However, the defection of Masinissa to the Roman cause shows that the Numidians could not be taken for granted and that the internal politics of the various contingents who comprised the Carthaginian army needed to be balanced, or at least held in check. The Moors (Mauri), in contrast, appear to have been on the fringe of, or beyond Carthage's hegemonic control, their kingdom being to west of the Numidians. Thus the Moorish light infantry deployed by Hannibal (Polybius 15.11.1, Livy 22.37.8-9) were mercenaries.

In Spain, as in North Africa, we see a similar mix. In those areas of the Iberian Peninsular under Punic rule, Carthage levied troops. Such levies were, of course, not always popular. During the Siege of Saguntum, the Oretani and Carpetani came near to rebellion over what Livy (21.11) describes as the 'severity of Hannibal's demands for troops'. Equally, following the successful conclusion to the siege, when Hannibal retired to winter quarters, he granted his Spanish levies leave prior to the invasion of Italy (Livy 21.21). Hannibal used the threat of the stick to overawe the wayward Oretani and Carpetani, and the carrot of leave prior to his great march. Such a judicious mix of punishment and reward appears to have kept those Spaniards who were subject to Carthage loyal, even to the extent of allowing Hannibal to dispatch, at the beginning of the war, Iberian levies to North Africa to help ensure the defence of the city. Daly has argued, given that Hasdrubal was, according to Diodorus (25.12), given the title of supreme commander (*strategos autokrator*) by the Iberians, that such loyalty was personal and vested in the body of the commanding Carthaginian, or more specifically Barcid, general. This may well be true, particularly as we are dealing with a warrior society, and as in all similar cases loyalty is vested in the person of the successful war leader, who in this case just happens to be a Carthaginian. Not all of Spain, by any means, was under Carthaginian control and troops from outside this area undoubtedly served as mercenaries rather than as allies – Livy and Appian both put Celtiberians and Lusitanians in Hannibal's invading force. The Celts and Ligurians of northern Italy had no reason to love Rome and numerous reasons to support Hannibal, but did they do so as allies or mercenaries? We just do not know. The answer is probably both. Hannibal forged formal alliances with a number of Celtic tribes and in the Hellenistic world such alliances were viewed as an excellent way of raising troops. Equally the successes of Trebia and Trasimene undoubtedly attracted what could be termed mercenary warbands eager for glory and plunder, while the chimerical success of Cannae caused a number of Italian towns and cities to defect to Hannibal. However, such defections in many ways limited his freedom of movement rather than increased his army, as few of these new allies were willing to provide troops to fight beyond the borders of their own territories.

# Hannibal's Army

## Military equipment

> He [Hannibal] ordered the Spaniards and the Africans and all the flower of his veteran army, taking their own baggage with them so as not to want the necessities of life wherever they might be forced to halt, to march in the van; the Gauls to follow them and form the centre of the column; and the cavalry to fall in behind. Mago and the Numidian light horse were to bring up the rear.
>
> Livy, XXII.ii.3-4

What then did this army look like? How were they equipped and how as a result did they kill? Did they shine like a river of steel, or like the earlier hoplites were they men of bronze? Did they all for that matter wear armour?

Military equipment creates not only the look and tactical repertoire of an army, it also in many ways defines our image of an army. Thus the Roman army of the first and second centuries AD will be forever viewed as one consisting of *lorica segmentata* clad legionaries delivering a *pila* volley before charging the enemy with *gladii Hispaneinsis*. Wellington's redcoats will always rise out of the corn at Waterloo, with bayonet tipped Brown Besses levelled ready to fire a devastating volley at close-quarters, followed by a bayonet charge which sweeps the enemy away.

The Carthaginians, however, apart from elephants, have no such clear-cut image and even with the (in)famous elephants there is no agreement, for as with the rest of the Carthaginian army we have debate – debate over the use of the *sarissa*, debate over the level of adoption of Roman equipment following Hannibal's victories at Trebia and Trasimene and debate over whether or not we should use Imperial Roman sources – particularly in relation to Trajan's Column and the Numidians. Finally there is debate over how Greco-Hellenistic the Carthaginian/Liby-Phoenician/African troops were in terms of weapons and armour (for soldiers, horses and elephants) during not only the Second, but also and particularly the First Punic War. However, aside from this, some areas of Hannibal's army are straightforward. The equipment of the Celtic, Celtiberian and Iberian troops is well understood and easily delineated, as indeed is the equipment, to a large extent, of those parts of Italy which defected to Hannibal (*colour plate 2*).

This discussion, based upon the division of the army into effectively national contingents, brings us to another point of departure, for the Carthaginian army does not follow the normal pattern of military equipment studies. There are of course no hard and fast rules for this, but one of a number of general patterns is usually followed. In the case of specific armies at set, usually short, points in time, we see a breakdown by troop type – infantry, cavalry, artillery, logistics, engineering etc, as, for example, in the case Duffy's study of Frederick the

## Units, Nationalities and Equipment

Great's army or Kemp's study of Marlborough's. Alternatively where a longer period of time is being studied, centuries as opposed to decades, then one of two breakdowns is followed, either chronological (see for example Bishop & Coulston, 2006) or by equipment type (see for example Stephenson, 2006). With the Carthaginian army none of these systems are terribly appropriate. Indeed the diverse nature of the Punic forces does not lend itself to such dissections. Rather it is easiest, with two exceptions, to describe and discuss the equipment employed by Hannibal's army in terms of national divisions. The same divisions, indeed, which we used to discuss and describe army organisation. We will therefore consider in turn the Africans, Spaniards or Iberians, Celts and Italians. The two groups which stand apart from such nationalistic groupings are the elephants and the skirmishers, who by nature of their more specialist tasks, fit and are as a consequence treated as, part of a more conventional breakdown.

## Elephants

When the Macedonian phalanx confronted the war-elephants of Porus at the Hydaspes River, in May 326 BC, they were faced with a frightening, even terrifying, yet as it turned out vulnerable opponent. For the beasts despite, as Arrian tells us (*Life of Alexander the Great*, V) causing frightful slaughter, at times to both sides, were wounded, exhausted and the survivors captured. As for the elephant riders, they were easily killed, for they sat on the animals backs armed with only a javelin or bow and although Porus is described as wearing armour, the rest appear not to have been so equipped and as a result were rapidly dispatched.

Moving forward to the mid-second century BC the elephant has gone from the exotic to the ordinary, becoming commonplace in the battle arrays of the Hellenistic successor states. Equally gone, other than the necessity of the mahout or driver (now armoured), are the warriors simply riding on the back of the elephant. In their place were towers carrying armoured archers or peltasts, as well as a *sarissa*-armed phalangite, with the Seleucids going even further and armouring the elephants themselves (*3*). Yet for all the undoubted splendour of the Seleucid elephants, by far the most famous of all the war elephants used in the ancient world were those deployed by Carthage and by Hannibal in particular (*colour plate 1*). However, fame has brought with it neither knowledge nor understanding.

The debate centres on the use of the tower by the Carthaginians and to some extent it seems straightforward. Alexander, following the Indian pattern, simply sat a mahout and an infantryman, specifically a phalangite, on the elephant's

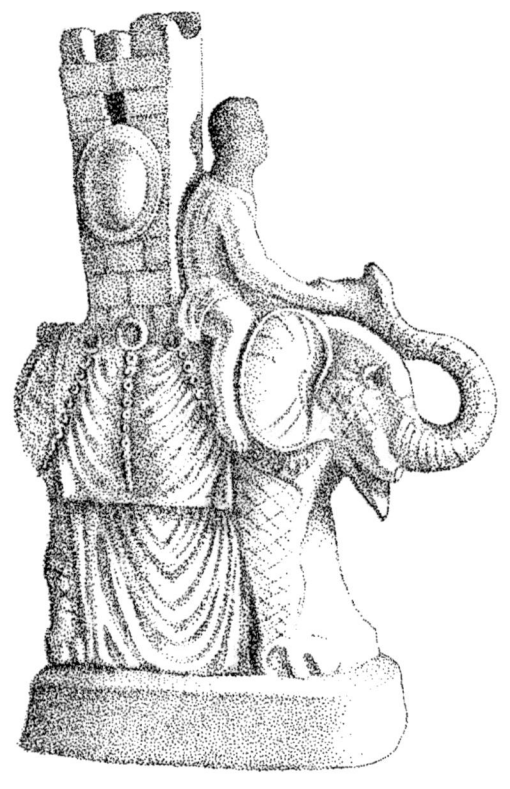

*3  The terracotta elephant figurine from Pompeii*

back. When the tower first appeared is uncertain; however, we do know that Pyrrhus, according to Zonaras (VIII.3) fielded elephants with towers against the Romans at Heraclea in 280 BC. This is their earliest attributed use and as a result their invention has at times been placed at Pyrrhus' door. Whatever the truth of the matter, towers, sensibly, in that they at least helped to protect the elephant's fighting crew, very rapidly became commonplace. In this context then it seems obvious that the Carthaginian's elephants were equipped with towers and certainly from the Renaissance onwards artists and historians have seen no reason to challenge this logic, particularly given the known historical interactions between Pyrrhus and Carthage. Doubts were, however, raised in the last century which have challenged this position.

The problem stems from the fact that the Carthaginians are now believed to have used African forest elephants – *Loxodonta africana cyclotis* – which unlike their larger bush cousins stood only some 7-8ft at the shoulder. Thus the problem, was the African forest elephant able to carry a tower and its crew? In opposition to the use of towers it has been argued that due to the animal's smaller size (it was also smaller than the Indian elephant which could bear a tower) it was not strong

## Units, Nationalities and Equipment

enough to carry both a tower and an armed contingent. Supporting this point of view we have the silence of Polybius and Livy on the subject, although *ex silentio* arguments cut both ways. More concrete evidence comes in the form of a number of Carthaginian, specifically Barcid, Spanish coins depicting elephants. None of them have towers and only one of them (possibly the most famous, a shekel from New Carthage, whose obverse bears a portrait of Hamilcar(?) as Melkart-Heracles) depicts a rider and then only a mahout.

In contrast the evidence for the use of towers is slightly more convincing. Leaving aside the *ex silentio* argument, we have the fact that Carthaginians encountered Pyrrhus' towered war-elephants. Equally the Ptolemaic army fielded towered African elephants, yet their war elephants were smaller than the bush variety and thus were in all probability the forest or *cyclotis* variety. Less circumstantially two Hannibalic silver coins from Campania have tower-bearing elephants on their reverse. Also from Campania – Cales to be specific – we have a *patera* which depicts an African and thus probably a Carthaginian elephant carrying a tower. The elephant and the tower depicted on the Cales *patera* is very similar to that of a terracotta figure from Pompeii which is believed to represent one of Hannibal's war elephants. Although slightly later, we have a clay loom-weight from Azaila, Spain, which shows a towered elephant and is probably intended to represent one of the 10 sent by the Numidian king Masinissa to Q. Fulvius Nobilior in support of his campaign against Numantia. Later still we read of towered elephants in the pages of Caesar's *African War* (30, 41 & 86).

The evidence is not overwhelming and can of course be read both ways, but the balance I believe is more in favour of the Carthaginians using towers than not, particularly given their association with Pyrrhus and the Hellenistic monarchies of the Eastern Mediterranean, all of whom used the latest technology and were at the cutting edge of military innovation. By the time of the Barcid intervention in Spain and certainly by the Second Punic War, for elephants that meant towers.

As to the form such towers took, while we see what might be an 'open' Ptolemaic tower, constructed of slats with gaps in between on an elephant figurine in the *Collection Fouquet* in Paris, we are probably on safer ground turning to the Cales *patera* and the Pompeii figurine, both of which show crenellated towers with a single, hoplite-style shield on the left (*patera* only) and right sides of the tower. In the case of the Pompeii find, the tower was decorated so as to appear to be made of stone and this probably reflects the reality of contemporary decoration.

Turning now to the capacity of these tower howdahs, they were undoubtedly smaller than those employed by the Selucids on their larger Indian elephants.

The Pompeii elephant bears an unarmoured mahout in front of an empty tower, while the Cales example again has a mahout, but this time the tower contains a solitary figure, although, obviously, with the *patera* we are only looking at one side of the elephant. One of the tiny silver coins from Campania is said to show three heads peeping over the top of the tower, but they could equally be crenellations. Given the smaller size of the elephant and the consequent reduction in carrying capacity, it seems likely that only two men were carried in the tower. This did, however, allow both sides to be fought simultaneously. It is also possible that helmets were worn, but that other forms of body-armour were eschewed in order to reduce the weight. As Carthage's elephants were designed to be used against infantry and cavalry, rather than against other elephants, then the crews would most likely have been armed with javelins, but their mahouts appear to have been unarmoured.

## SKIRMISHERS

> With a shout the auxiliaries rushed forward and the battle [Cannae] began between the light-armed troops.
>
> Livy, XXII.XLVII.1

Polybius (III.115) adds the fact that 'neither side had the advantage'. Yet in this context neither Livy nor Polybius describes the skirmishers' arms and armour. Plutarch in his *Life of Marcellus*, describing the death of the great general, tells us that the surprise attack which killed him opened with a shower of arrows – the enemy then closed in with spear and sword.

The skirmishers who fought in Hannibal's army and in the other forces that Carthage fielded, were drawn from the various contingents which made up such armies. They were thus like the body from which they were drawn – remarkably heterogeneous in nature, although in terms of their primary weapon they were a more, albeit not totally, homogeneous force. Plutarch's arrow shower, which does not appear in Polybius' or Livy's accounts of the death of Marcellus, stands as a rare use of the bow in the Punic Wars. The bow, although not completely unheroic, was not for that matter terribly heroic, nor was it, unless deployed in large numbers, a very effective battlefield weapon. Thus in this period battlefield archery was more a feature of Eastern Mediterranean warfare. Instead, as will be seen, the sling provided the Carthaginians with their main long-range missile capability.

However, for the vast majority of Hannibal's skirmishers the javelin was the primary weapon and these men should be viewed as Polybius' *longchophoroi* or spearmen. In terms of equipment, besides the javelin, armour and even helmets were probably not worn. Armour is of course no bar to movement, yet at this time it was restricted to close-order infantry. Shields, however, were carried. The Celts deployed light infantry at Telamon in 225 BC, but Polybius, who describes the battle (2.27-31), gives no detail as about their equipment. We are therefore left to speculate, remembering of course that warriors always fought with useable weapon sets. Thus besides the javelin (and more than one would have been carried, although probably no more than five – the maximum number that can be comfortably carried by hand without recourse to a quiver) any Celt, Celtiberian or Lusitanian skirmisher would have carried a shield and there is no reason to believe that it differed from those carried by their line counterparts (see below for details), as well as another weapon.

4   A Balearic(?) slinger on Trajan's Column. *Photograph C.M. Daniels*

*Hannibal's Army*

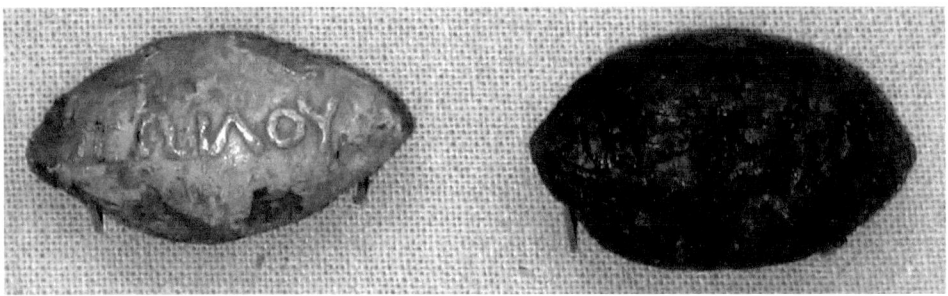

5  Lead slingshot in the British Museum. These examples are Greek, but are typical of the period

Head (1982) postulates a dagger, and certainly this makes sense, as some La Tène short swords or daggers as they have also been called, ranged in length from 29-55cm. Some may also have been armed with swords. North African (Numidian, Mauri and Libyan) and Iberian light troops would have been similarly armed. The Iberians were probably armed with a *falcata* (their version of the single-edged slashing sword which the Greeks called the *kopis*) while the North Africans will most likely have carried something like the double-edged short-sword (length 55-60cm) found in the second century BC Numidian Al Sumaa weapons grave. Unlike their Celtic colleagues, however, such troops were protected by smaller shields. In the case of the Spaniards this was the *caetra*, a bossed circular shield some 30-60cm in diameter, while Strabo (17.3.7) tells us that the Mauri used small, circular, boss-less rawhide (leather) shields. Marcellus was killed by a spear thrust and while it is quite possible to use a javelin in this way, the fact that the Al Sumaa grave contained two spearheads alongside the sword and javelins, suggests that some of Carthage's skirmishers may have been thus armed.

Today the Balearic slingers are remembered as some of the most famous specialist mercenaries in the ancient world (*4*). Initially hired for wine and women (they did not at first use money) the Balearians were allegedly able to shoot a stone slingshot weighing a *mina* or 436g (15.3oz) with great accuracy (*5*). How such large shot was carried is of course open to question. The famous 'Balearic' slinger on Trajan's Column carries his shot in his cloak, and this second century AD depiction may represent the reality of the Second Punic war. As for the slings themselves, Strabo (3.5.1-3) tells us that they were made 'of black tufted rushes [that is a species of rope rush out of which the ropes are woven] … or of hair or of sinew' and that the Balearians each carried a number of slings of different sizes so as to be able to hit targets at short, middle and long range.

Units, Nationalities and Equipment

## Celts

> The Insubres and Boii wore their trousers and light cloaks, but the Gaesatae had discarded these garments owing to their proud confidence in themselves, stood naked, with nothing but their arms, in front of the whole army.
>
> Polybius, 2.28.7-8

The Gaesatae at the Battle of Telamon in 225 BC present but one, albeit probably the best-known, image of the Celtic warrior – namely the naked champion with spiked lime white hair, armed with long-sword and shield, charging into battle. Of course this is not the whole picture, for at the other end of the spectrum we have the armoured chieftain splendidly arrayed in mail and helmet. In between these two extremes we see gradations of equipment.

The Celts – what exactly do we mean by this word? In this broad catch-all we include the Celtiberians from Spain, Gauls from the Po Valley and Cisalpine Gaul, as well as Ligurians from the Northern Apennines and the Italian Riviera. These peoples provided the Carthaginians with cavalry as well as infantry and despite the odd regional difference in equipment we see not only a commonality of style and form but an influence which spread beyond their bounds to Iberian, Roman and Italian areas of the Mediterranean (6).

Before, however, going on to describe what we do see, we shall begin by saying what we do not. The four-horned saddle, which was a Celtic invention and which became such a feature of Roman cavalry equipment, was not used

6  A Celtic cavalryman, from Magdalensberg

53

7  Infantry versus cavalry on the arch at Orange. *Photograph C.M. Daniels*

8  Cavalry combat. On the north relief of the Glanum monument. *Photograph C.M. Daniels*

in this period. It may appear on the first-century BC Gundestrup cauldron and it does appear on the arch at Orange (*7*) and on the St Rémy-de-Provence (Glanum) mausoleum (*8*), thus seeming to have originated in the first century BC and was not therefore a feature of Punic warfare.

All warriors, even the most naked of them, carried a shield into battle. As to the type of shield in general terms the form used, of a wooden board with a metal boss and a single central hand-grip, set the standard of shield design (and was copied with variety of course) up until the year AD 1000, when we see the introduction of the kite shield. In specific terms, in this period, such shields are described by Diodorus Siculus, Livy and Polybius. They appear in numerous works of art and are not an uncommon part of the archaeological record. Our breadth of knowledge stems not only from their ubiquity amongst their original masters, but also from the fact that successful designs, particularly in the field of military equipment, are copied, thus we see them in use in Spanish and Roman armies of the period.

In specific terms the shield itself was oval (*9*). The La Tène finds were on average 1.1m long and 0.6m wide at the centre, and made from three planks butted together (*10*). The Kasr el-Harit shield (a Ptolemaic-period Celtic-style shield from the Egyptian Fayum) was broadly similar, if slightly larger, being 1.28m long and 0.635m wide, but its construction was more complex, being fashioned from three layers of plywood. The board itself tended, although the practice was not universal, to be covered with leather, or lamb's wool felt in the case of the Kasr el-Harit find, which could be doubled over the rim to act as an edging. Metal edging is known but does not appear, archaeologically, to have been common. The central grip was horizontal with the hand being protected

*9* A currency bar, decorated with a Celtic shield, in the British Museum

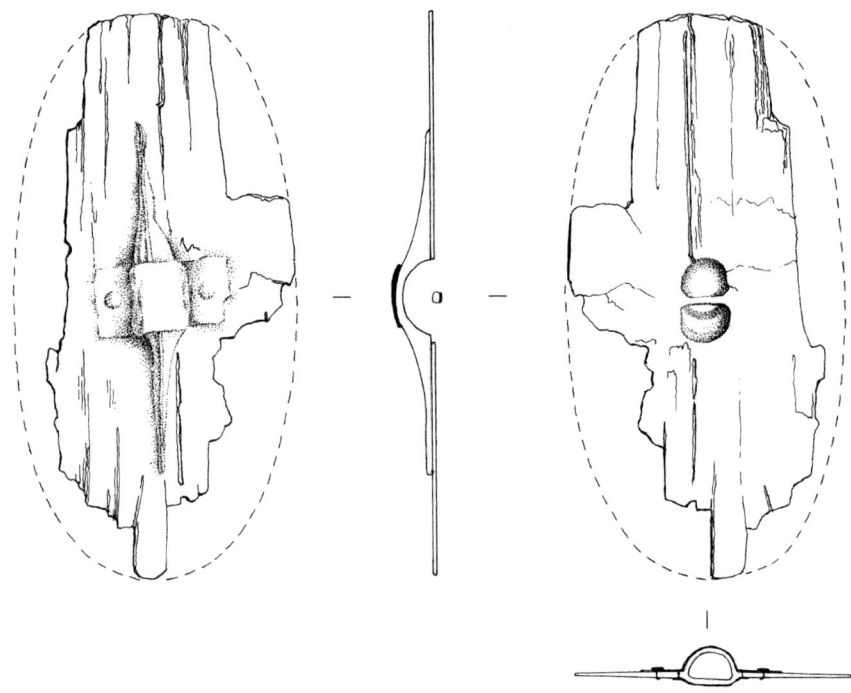

*10  One of the La Tène shields. Drawn by M. Daniels after Connolly (1978)*

by a long wooden 'spindle' or 'barleycorn' boss. Further protection for the hand was provided by an iron boss which overlay the centre of the wooden boss (*11; colour plate 13*). These iron bosses were riveted in place and took the form of either a simple strip or a slightly more complex winged variety.

Shield decoration is as ever problematic (*12*). Diodorus Siculus tells us that they were highly decorated and this should not surprise us in the least. Unfortunately no decoration survives archaeologically from the period of the Punic Wars. Surviving later British examples do not fit with the range of continental evidence, being at times far more elaborate, while the shield on the statue of a Gallic warrior from Mondragon, Vaucluse in France is simply decorated with a symmetrical lined pattern. Roman examples of Celtic shield patterns on, for example, the arch at Orange, suffer the same problems as Roman shield patterns on Trajan's Column and in the *Notitia Dignitatum*, in that we cannot ascribe patterns to units and we may at times be faced with artistic invention.

Body armour in the form of mail, another Celtic invention, was the preserve of the aristocracy. Daly (2002) places these armoured warriors purely amongst the cavalry, but heroic society does not work that way and while some would

Units, Nationalities and Equipment

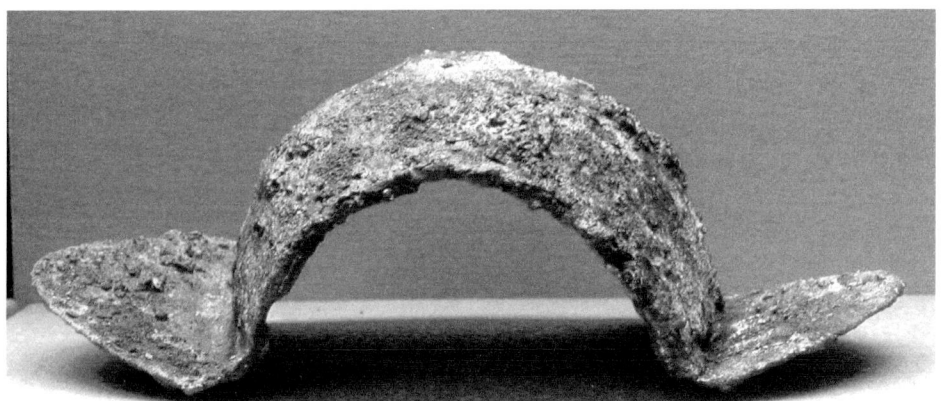

11   A cross-sectional view of a Celtic shield-boss, in the British Museum

12   Celtic shield patterns(?) on the arch at Orange. *Photograph C.M. Daniels*

*13 The Vachères warrior*

have led mounted contingents, others would have fought on foot, leading their men in the front rank of the infantry battle. As to the style of cuirass worn, the Vachères figure, the Aemilius Paulus and the Domitius Ahenobarbus reliefs all show mid- to upper-thigh-length shirts with shoulder-doubling (*13*). In these cases, and also in the case of the Pergamon reliefs, the shoulder-doubling takes the shape of the shoulder fastenings seen on earlier Greek and Hellenistic cuirasses. A more cape-like form of shoulder-doubling was also used, as can be seen for example on a statue of a Celtic warrior from Baratela in northern Italy. In all cases the mail would have been worn over a padded under-tunic, what the later anonymous Roman treatise *De Rebus Bellicis* called a *thoracomachus*.

Helmets would have been far more common than body-armour. They would not, however, have been universal. At this time the tall forms of earlier centuries had disappeared and the later styles, the forerunners of the Imperial-Gallic helmets, had yet to appear. Thus during the Punic Wars the plain iron or bronze Montefortino helmet predominated (*14*). More elaborate and more highly decorated versions of the basic Montefortino design existed; for the latter type see the helmets from Agris, Amfreville and Canosa in Feugère's *Casques Antiques* (1994), while one example of the more ornate style is the famous find from Ciume ti in Romania where the helmet was surmounted by a bronze bird whose hinged wings would have flapped as the wearer moved (*15*).

## Units, Nationalities and Equipment

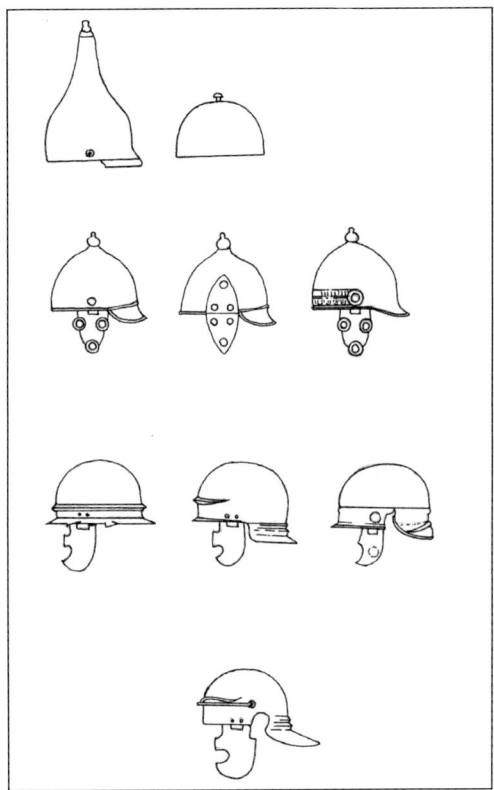

*Right* 14 Montefortino helmets (in the second row from the top) and their place in the evolution in Celtic helmet design. *Drawn by M. Daniels after Feugère (1994)*

*Below* 15 The Ciumeşti helmet. *Drawn by M. Daniels after Ritchie & Ritchie (1985)*

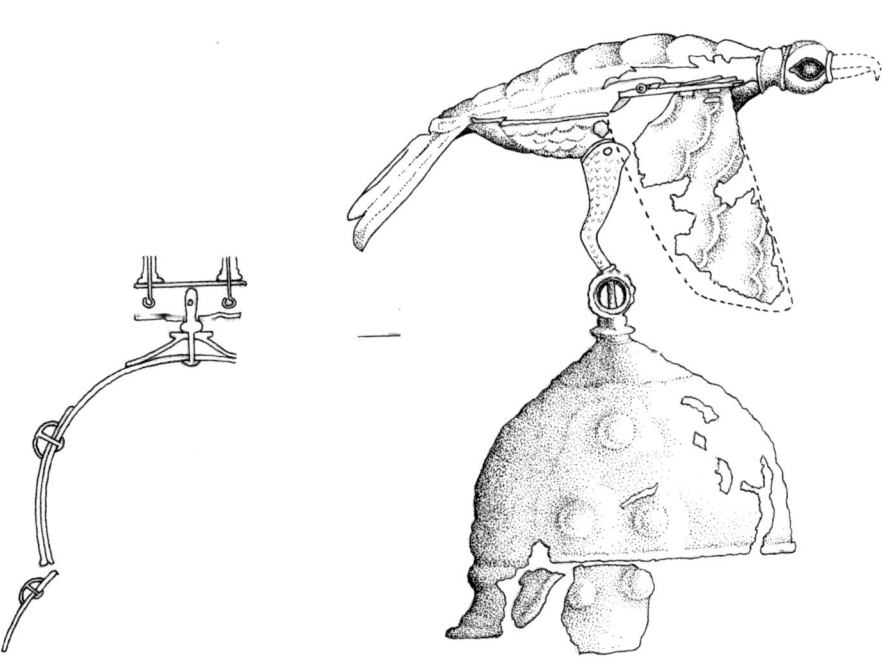

# Hannibal's Army

*16  A Celtic tanged javelin head in the British Museum*

Do we view the Celtic warrior primarily as a swordsman or a spearman? Certainly they used both weapons and it is equally certain that where they were equipped with a spear they also carried a sword, for the shield + spear combination on its own is not a viable weapons set.

The Celtic spear, and the same weapon was used by both infantry and cavalry, followed the Greek model. Spearheads were leaf-bladed, and both broad and narrow examples have been found (*16*). They could also be rather large with some examples being up to 50cm in length. Shafts were of ash, complete examples, as in most periods, are rare, but two complete finds from La Tène itself measured 2.5m (8ft 2in) in length, which in spear length terms appears to be rather the standard, as it accords with earlier Greek as well as later Roman and Germanic examples. It is thus highly probable that Celtic spears were all this sort of length. Their spears were also fitted with a butt-spike, the primary purpose of which was to act as a secondary spearhead if, or rather when, the first broke in combat. Such butt-spikes were conical and thus closer to later Roman types than to the square-sectioned Greek originals.

The Gaulish sword being only good for a cut and not a thrust.

From the way their [the Gauls] swords are made, as has been already explained, only the first cut takes effect; after this they at once assume the shape of a strigil, being so much bent both length-wise and side-wise that unless the men are given leisure to rest them on the ground and set them straight with the foot, the second blow is quite ineffectual.

Polybius II.30.8 & II.33.3

Despite Polybius' criticism, the Celtic double-edged iron long-sword remains a classic design and one which set the pattern for sword design well into the medieval period. Such swords had, according to Pleiner (1993), an average overall length (hilt + blade) of 72cm, with the range being between 55cm and 95cm. They were carried in metal sheet, either iron or copper-alloy, scabbards. The scabbards themselves could be very highly decorated and were suspended by a chain sword belt – baldrics were not used. Sword suspension was on the inner face of the scabbard and therefore against the body, a method Stead, in his 2006 work *British Iron Age Swords and Scabbards*, describes as 'suspension loops', while students of later periods would call them scabbard slides. All metal scabbards, as cavalrymen in the eighteenth and nineteenth centuries found, have their drawbacks. They were certainly more robust than their wooden counterparts, but whereas a sharpened blade kept in a wooden scabbard will retain its edge, the same blade in a metal scabbard will, with the constant movement of metal against metal, go blunt. A further potential drawback occurred where you had an iron sword in an iron scabbard, in that in wet weather the blade may become rusted into the scabbard.

Within this broad catch-all of Celtic, we of course see variations from the general picture. Thus the Ligurians fought predominately as infantry and particularly as light-infantry. They also, according to Diodorus (5.39.7), carried only medium length (72cm or shorter?) swords, while the Celtiberians followed their Iberian neighbours (see below) in using sinew greaves as well as single-edged and short-swords, the *falcata* and the *gladius Hispaniensis* respectively.

## IBERIANS

In their purple-edged dazzling white tunics, the Iberian levies who formed a part of the Carthaginian army must have looked striking indeed (*17* & *18*). Polybius (3.114.4) describes them as presenting 'a strange and impressive appearance'. Yet beyond this, as in so much of the military equipment of this period, we see evidence of overlaps of form and the beginnings of weapons whose later variants were used to more famous effect by Spain's Roman conquerors.

Sinew is the tough fibrous tissue connecting muscle to bone and from it the Iberian tribes made their helmets. Such helmets, as sculpture from Osuna in

Hannibal's Army

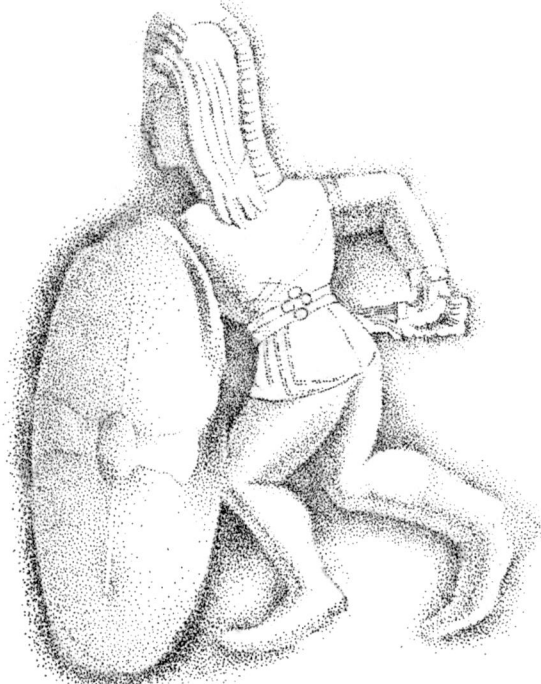

*Left* 17  An Iberian (Spanish) infantryman, armed with a falcata, and protected by a Celtic type shield and a crested sinew helmet

*Below* 18  An Iberian cavalryman from Cerillo Blanco de Porcuna. Of note is the *pectorale* and the shoulder guards

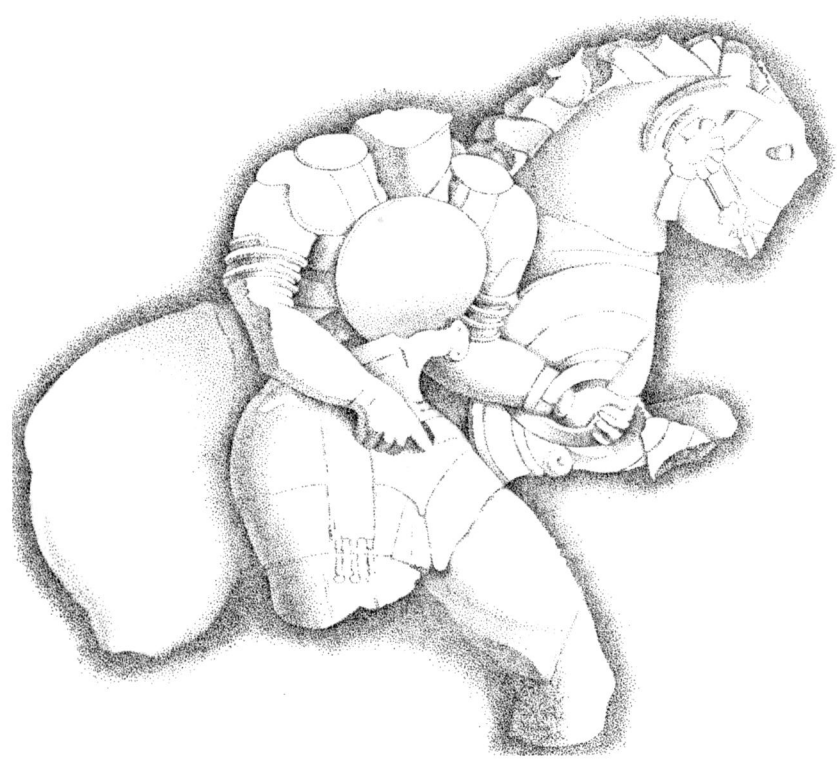

## Units, Nationalities and Equipment

southern Spain shows, could take the form of either simple caps or of longer hooded and crested forms which protected not only the head, but also the back of the neck. Body-armour was rare, but appears from the sculptural record to have consisted of a *pectorale* sometimes in conjunction with shoulder pads, for example as seen on the statue of a horseman in the Museo Arqueologico de Jaen. The *pectorale* or breastplate was a very simple form of armour consisting of a square, circular or trilobate copper-alloy plate which, held in place by a series of straps, protected the wearer's chest.

Two types of shield were used. The line infantry used the oval Celtic shield. The light infantry and the cavalry used the *caetra*, which as has already been described, is a small round shield held by a single central hand grip, yet also carried at the same time by a shoulder strap (*19*). In terms of shield usage we see the Iberian troops very much in line with prevailing military practices, in that the line infantry generally favoured a large oval shield, while light infantry and cavalry very much tended towards the use of a smaller circular shield. In all of these cases we see centre-grip shields.

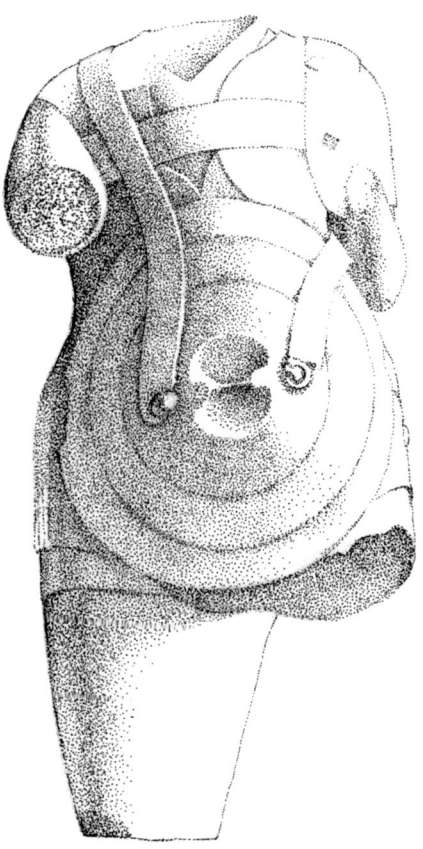

Along with the two different types of shield, we also see two different types of sword in use, however, where we can draw demarcation lines for shield use the same cannot (nor indeed does it need to be) done for the swords, as both types were equally usable on horse or foot. The *falcata* or *espada falcata* as it is also sometimes referred to in modern works, appears to have been the more common of the two types used (*20*). The weapon itself was in effect nothing more than a variant of the Greek *kopis*, namely a single-edged weapon with a blade length of 35-52cm. Designed predominantly as a slashing sword, the point and back-edge of the

*19* This third-century BC sculpture nicely illustrates not only the *caetra's* layered construction, but also the shield's central grip and its shoulder strap.

63

Hannibal's Army

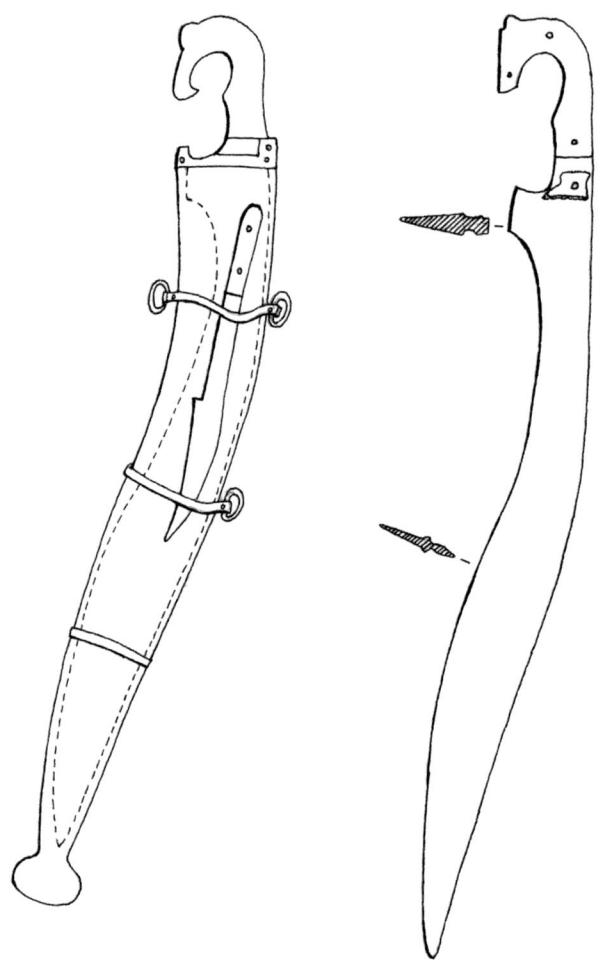

20 The falcata and its associated dagger. *Drawn by M. Daniels after Quesada Sanz (1997)*

point were also sharpened allowing it to thrust as well as cut. Worn on a baldric and suspended at the waist and across the front of the body, the *falcata* was short enough not to require being worn on either hip. At times we see a short dagger attached to the front of the weapon's scabbard.

Polybius (3.114) views the Spanish sword, the forerunner of the *gladius Hispaniensis*, as equally good at cutting and thrusting. Such weapons were double-edged with a sharp, tapering point. Although very similar in basic shape to La Tène period II swords, the Spanish sword was, however, shorter, being only some 60cm in length. Carried in a sometimes highly decorated scabbard, it was worn suspended on the right-hand side by a baldric and suspension loops (*21, 22 & 23*).

Iberian *scutarii* or line infantry, were so-called for their large Celtic-style oval shields, carried along with a sword and a heavy javelin (*colour plate 3*). The

*1  A Carthaginian war elephant – Second Punic War*

2  A Celtic warrior – Second Punic War

3  An Iberian *scutarii* – Second Punic War

4  Italian infantryman/Roman legionary – Second Punic War

5   Numidian cavalryman – Second Punic War

6  Carthaginian cavalryman – Second Punic War

7  Libyan infantryman – Barcid Spain

*8* A Hellenistic period helmet from the tomb of Lyson and Kallikles

9   The monument commemorating the Battle of Trasimene

*10* Looking towards Lake Trasimene from the monument. Hannibal concealed the bulk of his army in the rolling countryside which rises up from the lake

*11 A detail of the Numidian/Mauri cavalry on Trajan's Column. Photograph C.M. Daniels*

*12* A terracotta figurine of a Hellenistic period heavy cavalryman, in the British Museum

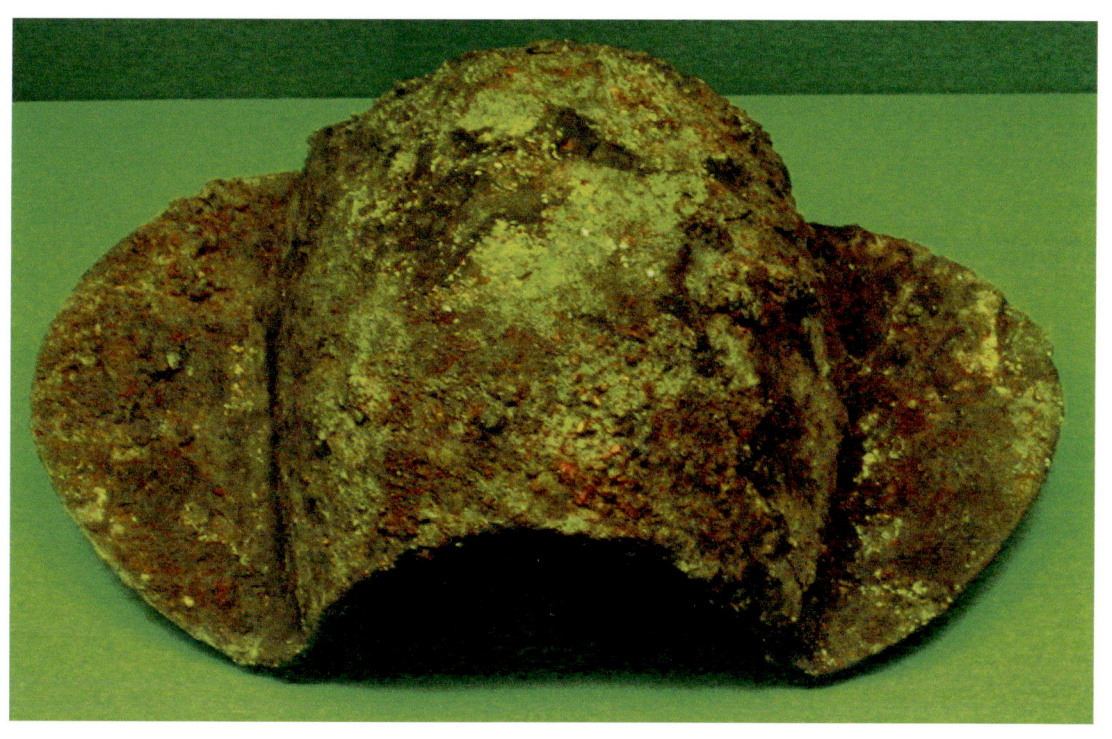

*13* A La Tène period II iron shield-boss, in the British Museum

14　Reconstructions of third- and second-century BC Roman Republican weapons

15 The carrying system employed on the phalangite's shield

16 The *sarissa* in action

*Units, Nationalities and Equipment*

21 The tang of a La Tène period II sword, in the British Museum

23 The chape from the scabbard of a La Tène period II sword, in the British Museum

22 The sword suspension loop on a La Tène period II sword, in the British Museum

## Hannibal's Army

*soliferreum* was an iron spear about 1.6-2.0m in length. The iron shaft was round in cross-section and approximately 1cm in diameter. It had a small barbed head and a pointed butt. At close range, and it was undoubtedly a close-range weapon, it would have possessed a great deal of penetrative power.

The Saguntines used a weapon:

> ... called a *falarica*, with a shaft of fir, which was round except at the end whence the iron projected; this part, four-sided as in the *pilum*, they wrapped with tow and smeared with pitch. Now the iron was three feet long, that it might be able to go through both shield and body. But what chiefly made it terrible, even if it stuck fast in the shield and did not penetrate the body, was this, that it had been lighted at the middle and so hurled, the flames were fanned to a fiercer heat by its very motion, and it forced the soldier to let go his shield, and left him unprotected against the blows that followed.
>
> Livy, XXI.VIII.10-12

Livy's description is colourful, and similar weapons were used in Spain in the thirteenth century AD during the Reconquista. However, at this later date they

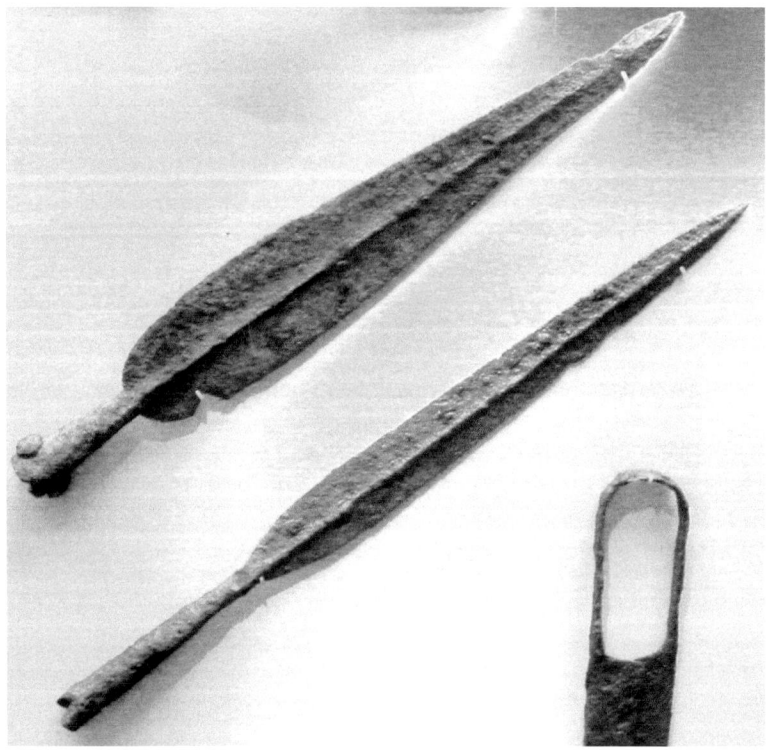

24 Two La Tène period II spearheads in the British Museum

were used in siege warfare and this should be when we would expect to see the incendiary aspect of Livy's *falaricas*. On the field of battle they were probably used in a more prosaic armour-piercing capacity. Iberian cavalry, like their Celtic contemporaries carried a long thrusting spear. As with the La Tène finds, leaf-shaped heads up to 50-60cm in length were not unknown (*24*).

## ITALIANS

Cannae saw the defection of a number of Southern Italian towns to Hannibal, but this did not providing a massive net gain in troops for the Carthaginians, as some saw it merely as a means to break with Rome and would therefore fight only in their own defence. However, others fought alongside Hannibal, even going so far as to follow him to ultimate defeat and destruction at Zama (*colour plate 4*).

Rome, ordering all things to its will, required her allies to supply troops (infantry and cavalry). Expected to fight alongside the city's own citizen soldiers, such troops were equipped after the Roman style. At some point in the Republican-period Roman cavalry equipment was reorganised along Greek lines. Unfortunately Polybius (6.25.3-11), who describes the process, fails to date it and as a result there is no consensus amongst modern commentators as to when it occurred. Thus dates have varied from the fourth century through to the second century BC. Before going on to look at when it occurred and the implications, if any, for southern Italian cavalry fighting for Hannibal, we must first answer the question – what equipment exactly are we talking about?

At one point Polybius tells us that Roman, and by extension allied, cavalry fought unarmoured with only inadequate ox-hide shields for protection, while for offence they used a decidedly poor design of spear, which had a shaft that was too thin and lacked a butt-spike. Then at some point this all changed. Roman cavalry became armoured, adopted a sturdier shield and a spear with a more substantial shaft as well as a butt-spike – in other words they were armed along Greek lines.

As to when such a change probably occurred, McCall (2002) is undoubtedly correct in arguing that motive is required. I further agree with him that the best motive stems from the debacles of the early years of the Second Punic War. However, it is also possible that the towns and cities of southern Italy, given their contact both with Sicily and Greece, had already, although not in a universal way, begun to adopt aspects of Greek-style cavalry equipment. Thus we would expect to see Boeotian helmets, a degree of body armour, either mail, stiffened-

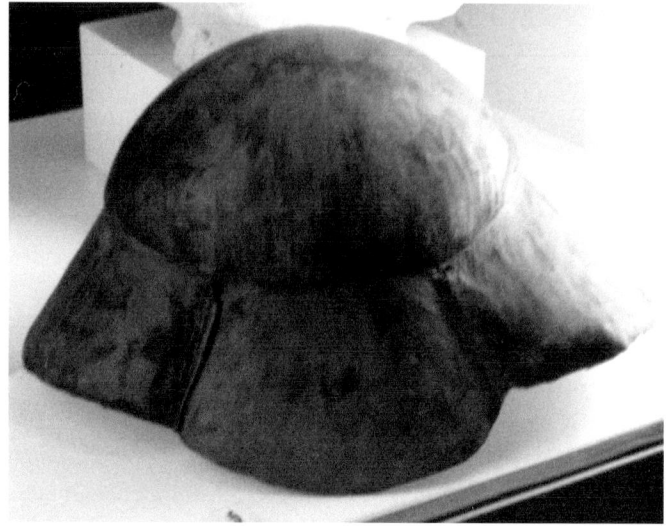

25 A Roman Boeotian style cavalry helmet, in the Rijksmuseum van Oudheden in Leiden

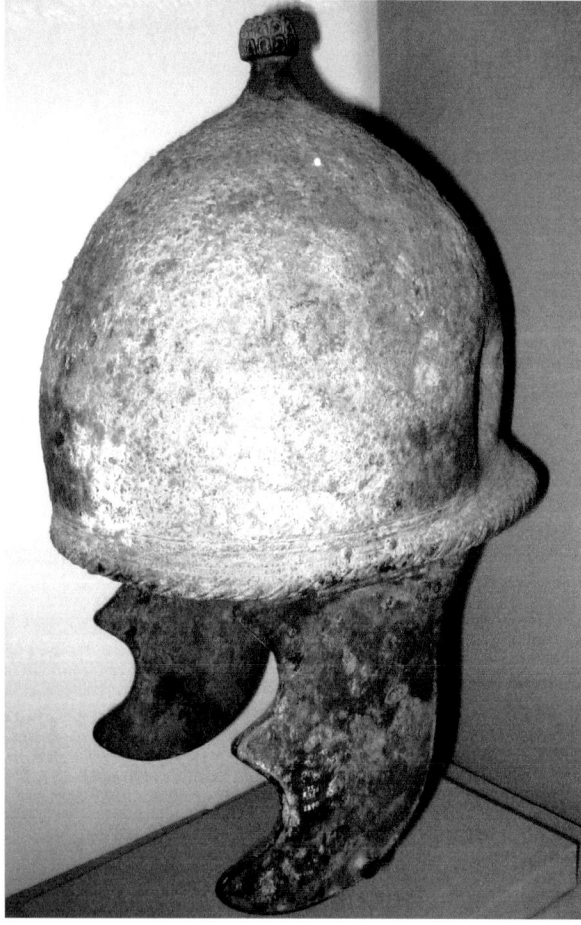

26 A Roman example of a Montefortino helmet, in the British Museum

## Units, Nationalities and Equipment

linen or muscled cuirasses, as well as circular wooden shields along with more substantial, butt-spiked spears (*25*). Indeed the process in the south may have been accelerated by their incorporation into Hannibal's army, accompanied as it was by the spoils of Cannae.

The Italian infantry who fought for Carthage would have been equipped after the manner of the Roman legionaries of the day. Roman legionary fashion, not just in this period but in the centuries to come, was based upon techno-borrowings, in that it was derived in terms of form and function from earlier and current enemies. Thus we would see Celtic-style shields and Montefortino helmets, along with double-edged Spanish style swords (*26, 27 & 28*). As to the type of body-armour worn, that was very much dependent upon wealth and social status. The poorest troops would have been simply armoured with *pectorales*, whereas those who fulfilled the relevant property qualifications were expected to, and undoubtedly did, wear either mail (after the Celtic fashion with shoulder-doubling) or a bronze muscled cuirass. In all cases under-armour padding was worn. With the muscled cuirass and the mail shirt this took the form of a full, separate garment, whereas with the *pectorale*, as an example from Numantia suggests, the padding was attached to and formed a backing to the armour itself (*29*).

Alongside those pieces of military equipment which we have already encountered, we find others which were used by Roman, Latin and Italian troops and, as a consequence of victories in Spain and Italy during the early years of the Second Punic War, were also used by the Carthaginians themselves.

*27* A detail of the hinge used to suspend the cheek-piece on a Montefortino helmet, in the British Museum

Hannibal's Army

28 The back of a Montefortino helmet. Note the very small neck guard

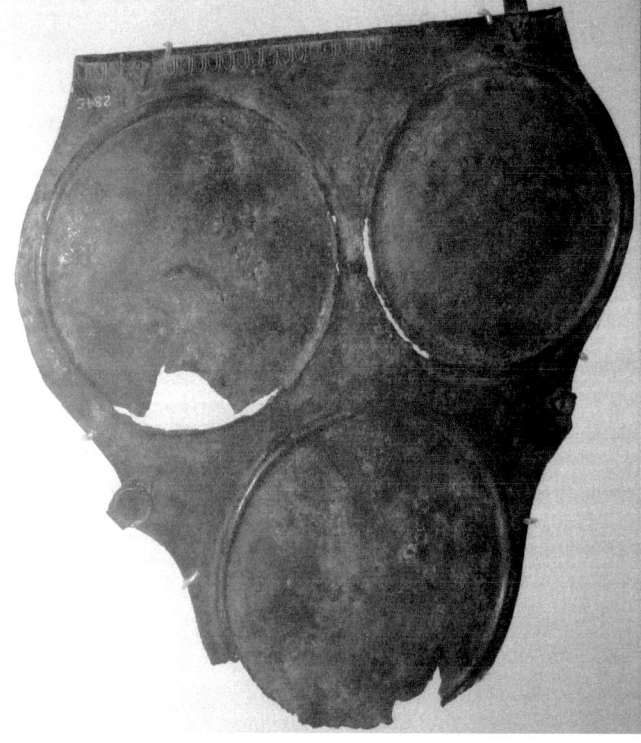

29 The simplest form of armour – a trilobate *pectorale*. This example is in the British Museum

*Units, Nationalities and Equipment*

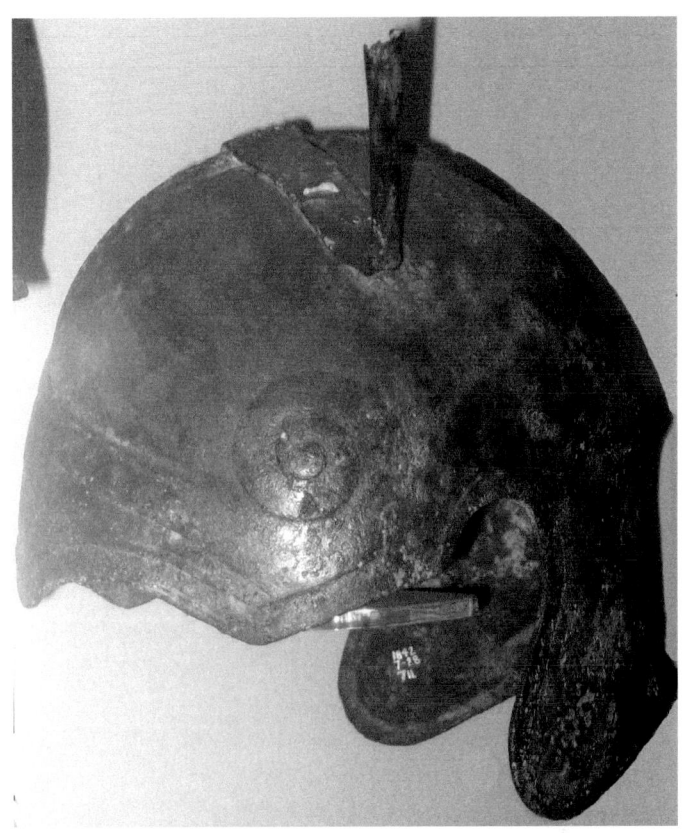

*30 A Roman Attic helmet, in the British Museum*

*31 A Roman Etrusco-Corinthian helmet, in the British Museum. This type of helmet, along with the Attic helmet in 31 would originally have been fitted with cheek-pieces*

# Hannibal's Army

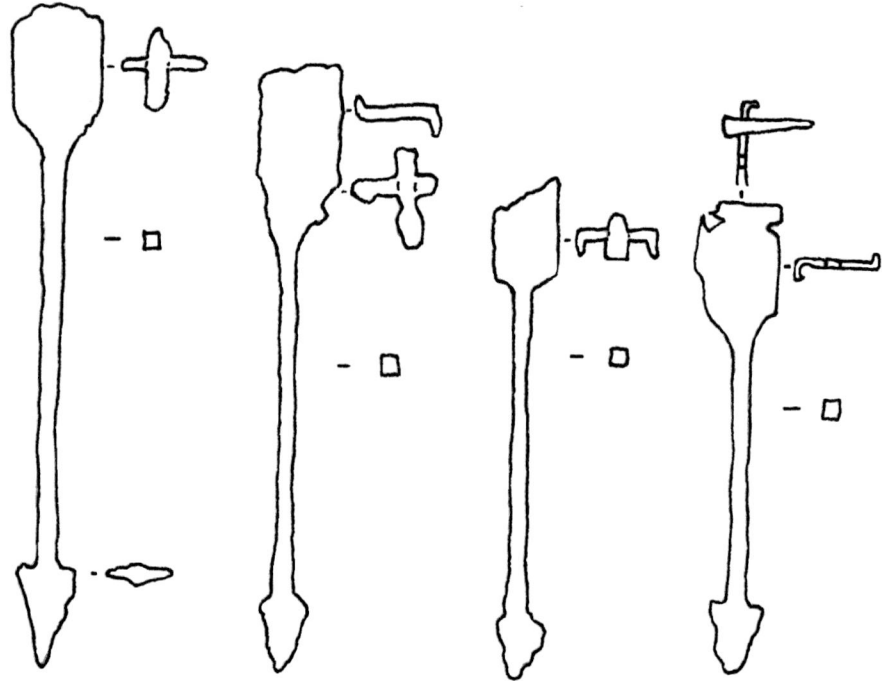

32  *Pila* heads from Telamon. *Drawn by M. Daniels after Sekunda 1996*

Thus amongst the ranks of the Punic forces we would find soldiers wearing Attic and Etrusco-Corinthian helmets (*30* & *31*). We would also see the Italians and, most probably, the Iberians equipped with *pila* (*32*). The *pilum* (plural – *pila*) was, of course, the famous Roman armour-piercing heavy javelin. The question of whether or not Hannibal rearmed his Libyan infantry with *pila* and trained them after the Roman manner is discussed in Chapter 5.

Finds of *pila* from this period of Republican history are rare and indeed such finds as there are are uncertain in date. A number, around 60, have been found at Telamon, and may well date from the battle fought there in 225 BC. The Telamon finds were between 18.8 and 35cm in length and had small barbed heads.

## Africans

Of all the groups that together made up the armies of the Carthaginian state, the most problematic are the Africans themselves. For although we can easily name the main ethnic groups – Numidians, Mauri, Libyans, Liby-Phoenicians

# Units, Nationalities and Equipment

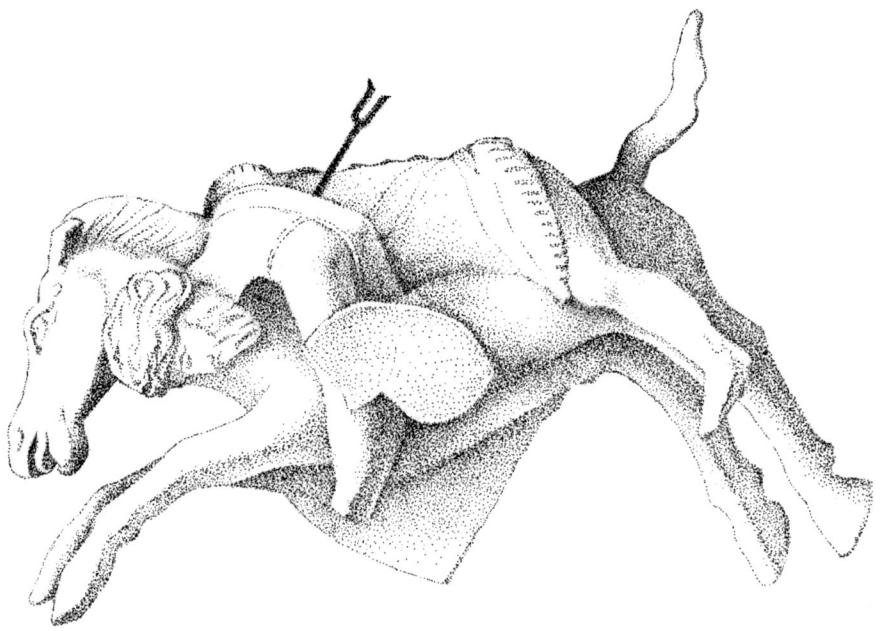

*33  A third-century BC terracotta statue of a Numidian warrior, from southern Italy*

and Carthaginian citizens, we run into the usual evidence problems when we attempt to define and describe their equipment (*33*). Therefore, at times, when attempting to arm, particularly Hannibal's North African infantry, later writers have imposed what can only be described as a best fit based upon the prevailing Hellenistic military trend, while in the case of the Numidians, and as a consequence the Mauri, the exclusion of later evidence would leave us with virtually nothing.

Appian (*The Punic Wars*, 11) tells us that the Numidians were trained, day and night, to hurl showers of javelins from horseback and certainly this is the image, reinforced by Caesar, Virgil, Livy and Arrian of such troops in popular imagination. These horsemen, Numidians and Mauri or Moors, are described by later sources and depicted on Trajan's Column where they are lightly clad, wearing only a tunic and protected by a simple circular shield, while their horses lack bit and bridle (*34; colour plates 5 & 11*). Livy (XXII.48) also has them armed with swords, which they could conceal, and this image has to some extent been confirmed archaeologically by the second century BC Al Sumaa weapons grave, which contained alongside javelins with both square and round cross-sectional heads, a short sword with a blade length of approximately 60cm.

*Hannibal's Army*

*34 Numidian/Mauri cavalry on Trajan's Column. Photograph C.M. Daniels*

If such troops provided Hannibal and the Carthaginian state with its light cavalry, then the heavy, close-order shock cavalry was provided by the Celts and Spaniards, who we have already discussed, as well as by the Libyans and the Liby-Phoenicians. While in the case of the latter group, the Liby-Phoenicians, there is, as Daly (2002) points out, no evidence that they ever fought as anything other than cavalry.

A terracotta disc from a tomb in the Douimès district of Carthage, which may be slightly earlier in date than the period of the Second Punic War, points to the fact that such cavalry was undoubtedly equipped after the Greek fashion and unlike their lighter counterparts employed bit, bridle, and reins (*35, 36 & 37; colour plate 6*). The figure on the disc, as can be seen in the illustration, is armed with a thrusting spear, wearing a crested helmet and carries what in a Roman context would be described as a *popanum* shield (so named by Polybius (6.25.7) because they resembled 'the round, bossed cake used in sacrifices'). Indeed he is very like the figure of Marcus Curtius as depicted in a relief in the Palazzo dei Conservatori. As well as the *popanum*-type shields we might also expect to see more Greek-style circular cavalry shields, with a central 'barleycorn' spine and metal shield boss. The rider would in all probability have been armoured with a helmet and body-armour, which will be discussed further in the section on

Units, Nationalities and Equipment

35 The Greek style of cavalry, as depicted on a vase in the British Museum. Of note besides the thrusting spear is the bronze muscled cuirass

36 A Carthaginian cavalryman as depicted on a terracotta plaque from the Douimes district of Carthage

## Hannibal's Army

*37 A figurine of a Hellenistic period light cavalryman, in the British Museum*

infantry equipment below. However, in this context, it is worth pointing out that the spoils of war would have provided Carthage's cavalry with a number of Boeotian-style helmets. As well as the thrusting spear, which would have been some 8ft in length and fitted with a butt-spike, such cavalrymen would also have carried a sword, which we shall also discuss in the context of the infantry.

In many ways the question of how the Libyan infantry were armoured is the easiest question to answer (*colour plate 7*). Helmets derived from two distinct sources and there would be the same styles worn by the Numidian nobility. Thus on the one hand we would expect to see Macedonian (Hellenistic) styles,

## Units, Nationalities and Equipment

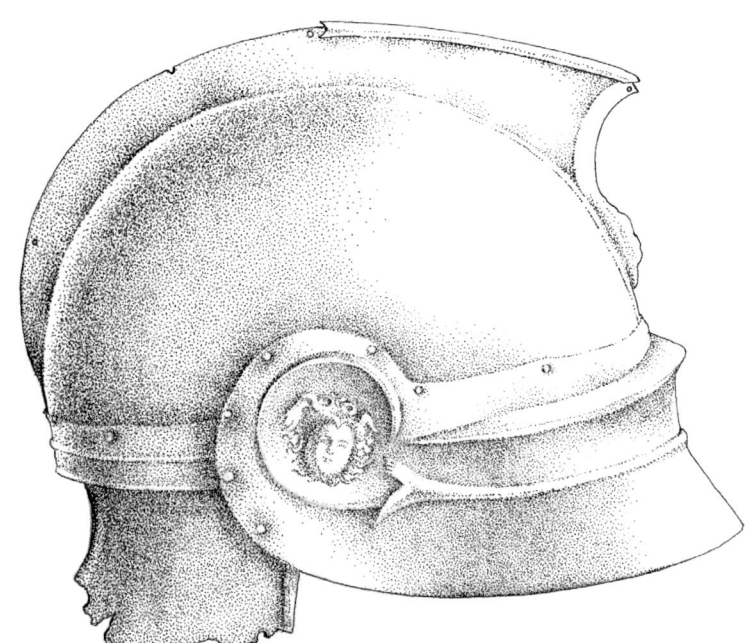

*38* The Hellenistic Melos helmet, side view

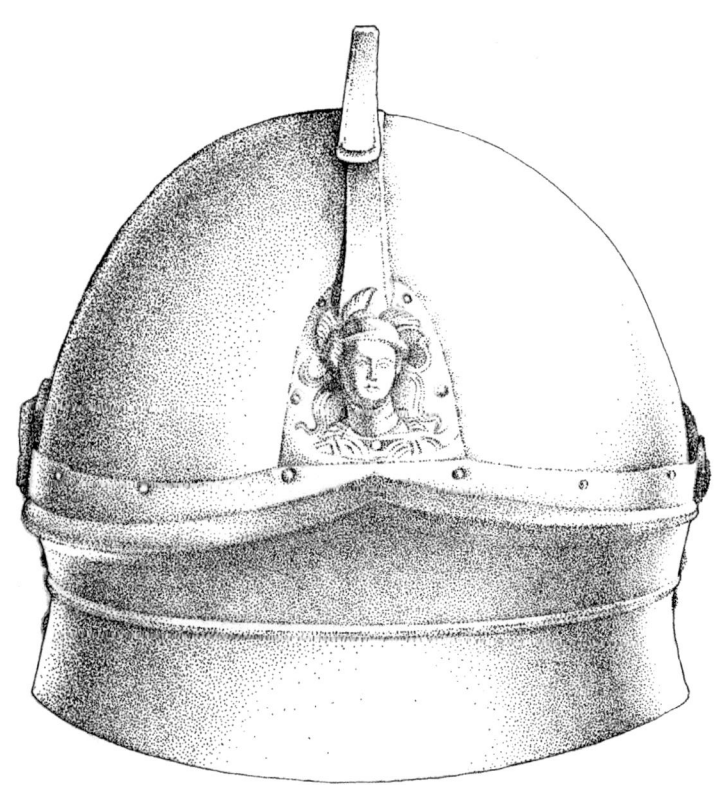

*39* The Melos helmet as seen from the front

*Hannibal's Army*

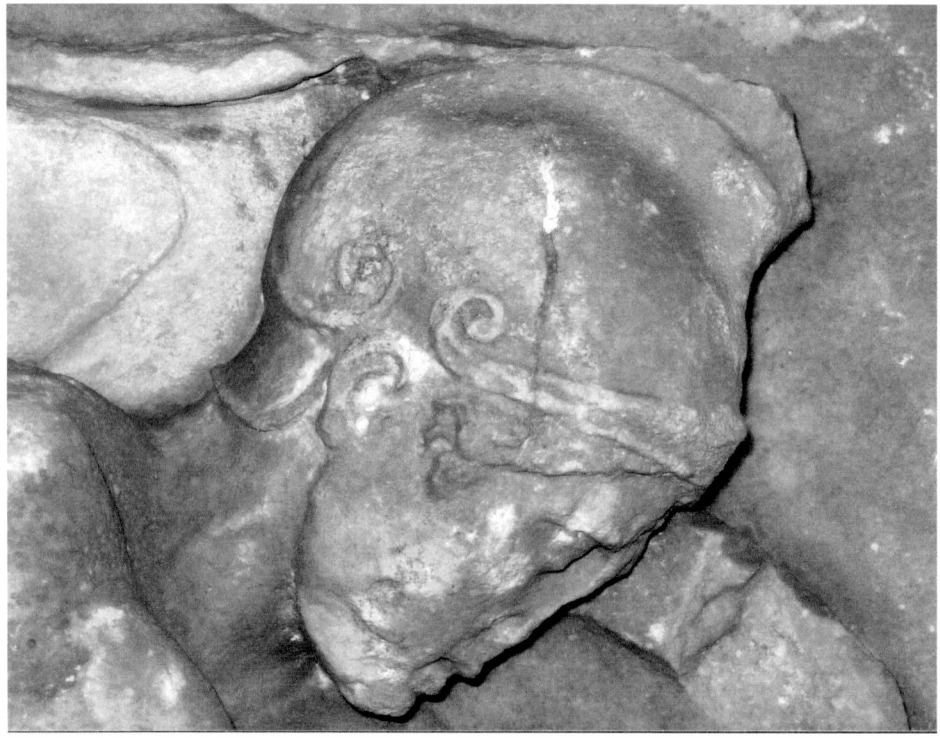

*40  An early example of what would become the Hellenistic style. This helmet is on the Amazon frieze from the Mausoleum at Halikarnassos in the British Museum*

typified by the frescos in the *c*.200 BC tomb of Lyson and Kallikles (*colour plate 8*), from Edessa, northern Greece, and by extant finds such as the Melos helmet and a similar example now in the Hermitage, St Petersburg (*38, 39 & 40*). The helmets so beautifully executed on the walls of the tomb of Lyson and Kallikles are painted in reds, blues and yellows, and although this could so easily be dismissed as artistic license, the fact remains that actual metal helmets were painted well into the late medieval period in order to increase the splendour of their appearance. We are thus, in all probability, seeing the same thought process at work here, although as with later periods it would be going too far to argue that all such helmets were painted.

The remains of a helmet from Al Sumaa points to and defines the antecedents of the second strand of Punic helmets (*41*). The Al Sumaa helmet was, when new, conical. It was thus just one in a line of helmets whose ancestry stretched back to Carthage's Phoenician homeland and beyond to the Middle East and the Assyrian Empire (*42*). The Al Sumaa helmet was definitely in the same tradition and in fact followed the later practice of such helmets in having integral

## Units, Nationalities and Equipment

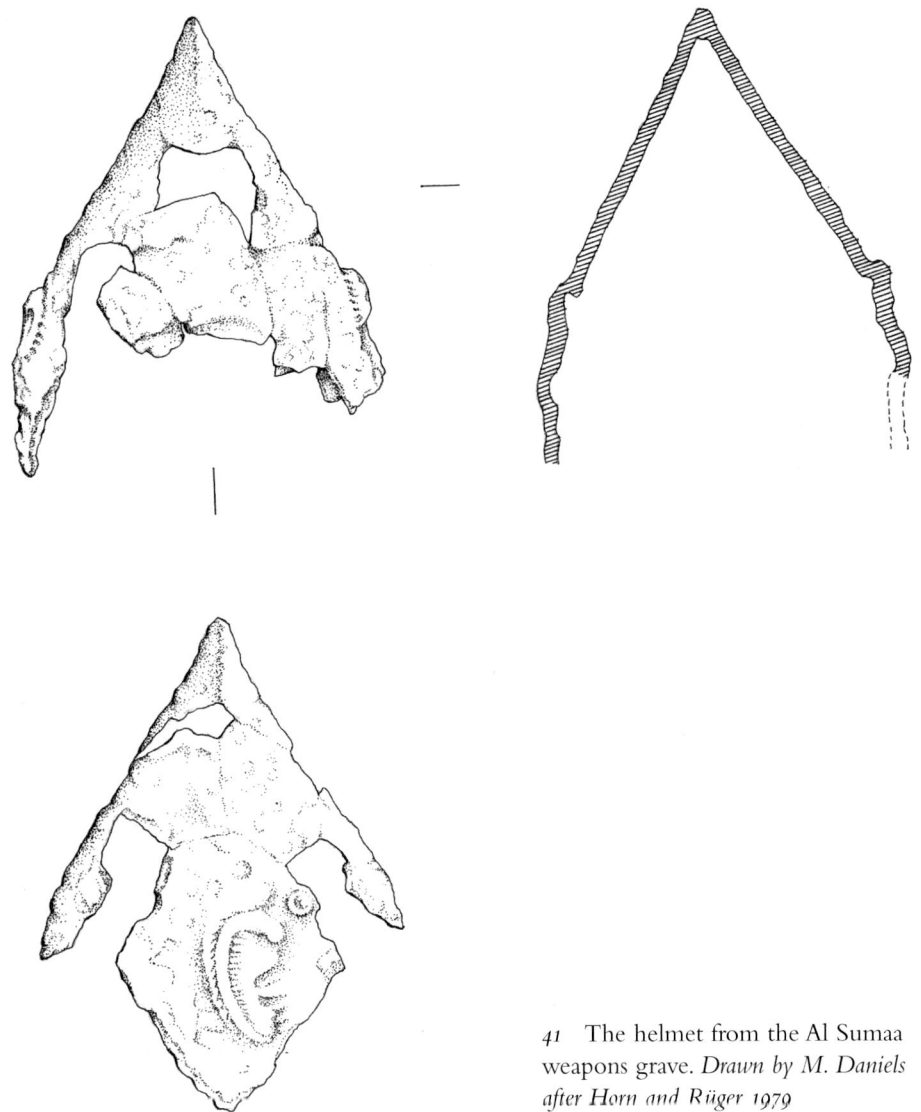

41 The helmet from the Al Sumaa weapons grave. *Drawn by M. Daniels after Horn and Rüger 1979*

cheek-pieces, or possibly ear protectors, in that each side was decorated with an imitation ear.

We gain the impression from the stripping of the Roman dead, particularly after the Battles of Trebia and Trasimene, that the Carthaginians were less well armoured than their enemy. How true this actually was is difficult to ascertain. What we should perhaps accept is that like their Roman counterparts, different social groups within the ranks of the Libyan infantry had different levels of body-armour. Equally to the victor go the spoils

*42  An Assyrian forerunner of the Al Sumaa helmet, from a relief in the British Museum*

*43* A muscled cuirass on the fourth century BC tomb of Payava in Xanthos, in the British Museum

## Hannibal's Army

– victorious soldiers have always 'upgraded' their equipment by looting the dead and the wounded.

A highly ornate trilobate *pectorale* from the Ksour-es-Sad tomb in Tunisia stands as probably the best-known piece of armour associated with Hannibal's army, best-known in that although it is believed to be Italian in origin, its final resting place has meant that it is usually interpreted as belonging to a soldier in Carthage's service. Alongside such highly decorated examples we would also expect, and have indeed found, plainer contemporaneous examples. A greater degree of protection was provided by the muscled cuirass and this also provided a measure of continuity with the First Punic War, where this piece of armour was used by the Romans and the Carthaginians (*43*). A feature of art well into the Imperial Roman period, muscled cuirasses were at this time still a practical piece of military equipment (*44*). Generally these were waist length,

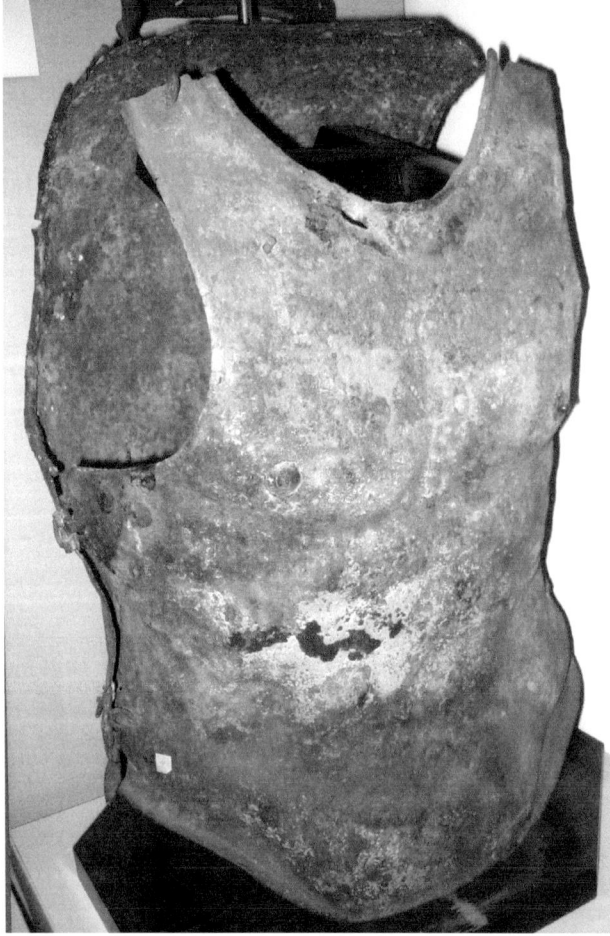

*44* A bronze muscled cuirass in the British Museum, note the simple shoulder and side fastenings

## Units, Nationalities and Equipment

45 Protection for the modern rider. This updated version of the muscled cuirass is worn by my god-son Ross Mayes

although it has been argued that the frescos in the tomb of Lyson and Kallikles point to the existence of shorter examples, which may be a cavalry adaptation designed to protect without discomforting the rider (a modern version of this style of protection is regularly worn by riders today (45)). A number of reliefs from Simitthus-Chemtou monument in Tunisia show sleeveless body-armour with shoulder-doubling and *pteruges* (the skirt of protective strips) along the bottom edge (46). These reliefs could, as some have argued, represent mail, but equally they could possibly show rigid linen corslets, or, and this is less likely due to their rareness, they could show iron cuirasses similar to that found in the tomb of Philip II of Macedon at Vergina. The most likely explanation is that they show either mail or rigid linen armour, both of which would have been worn by Libyan infantry and cavalry (47). Greaves were worn,

46 Under-armour padding with *pteruges*, detail from a statue in the Museo della Terme, Rome. *Drawn by M. Daniels after Robinson 1975*

47 A linen(?) cuirass on a funerary relief from Canosa, northern Apulia, now in the British Museum

*Units, Nationalities and Equipment*

and where worn would have been the snap-fit variety which we associate with the Greeks (*48*). The question of the type of shield used is more vexed, being determined by the infantryman's primary weapon and as a result this will be discussed in that context. However, alongside his primary weapon each soldier also carried a secondary weapon.

The spear, in one form or another, formed the primary weapon for the vast majority of soldiers from the Hoplite Revolution through until at least the Middle Ages. On its own, however, it was not viable, as the spear is a distance killer. Even if that distance is only some 6ft, it is still unusable at true close-quarters, when the enemy is only 1-2ft away, and it must therefore form a part of a weapons set. Thus if the spear in one form or another was the primary weapon, then the sword in one form or another was the secondary weapon. For the sword was very much a close-quarters weapon.

Carthage's long and close association with Spain undoubtedly resulted in the adoption, by at least some of the city's North African troops, of the double-edged Spanish sword (*49* & *50*). Equally the *kopis*, or *machaira* as it is also termed, the single-edged slashing sword which first appeared in Greece in the sixth century BC and spread around the Mediterranean, would also have been used (*51*). Straight,

*48* Greek snap-fit bronze greaves in the British Museum

Hannibal's Army

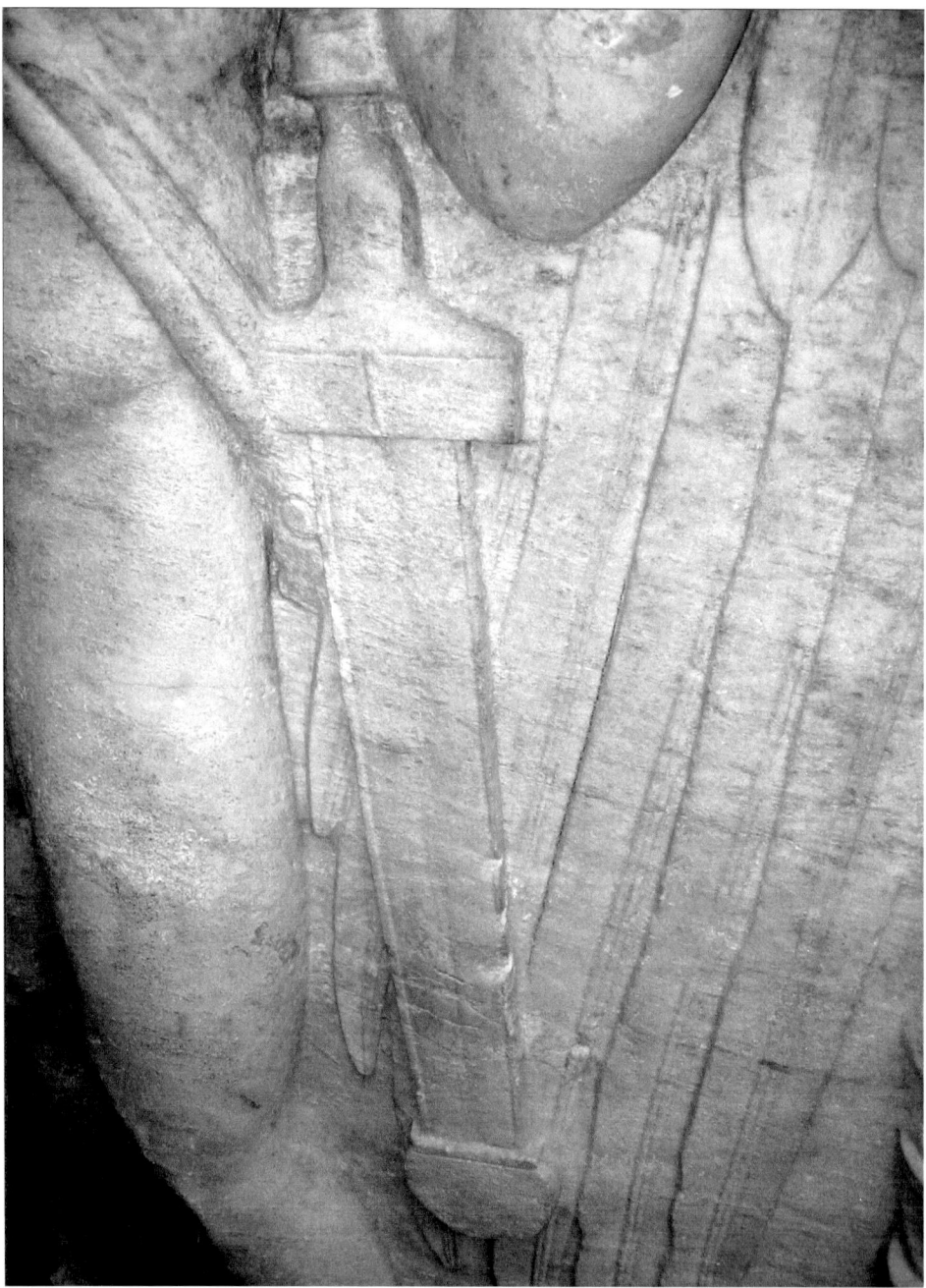

49 An alternative to the *kopis*, the double-edged sword, on a Hellenistic-period relief in the British Museum

Units, Nationalities and Equipment

50 A detail of the hilt of the sword in 49

Macedonian-style swords, such as those featured on, amongst other things, the Pergamon frieze and a Hellenistic-period relief in the British Museum would have completed the range of swords available to Carthage's Libyan infantry.

That the Libyans were once equipped as, and fought as, hoplites is not in question, whether or not they still did so during the Second Punic War is open to debate. According to Plutarch's *Life of Timoleon* at the Battle of the Crimisus River in 339 BC (between the Carthaginians and a Sicilian Greek force led by Timoleon) the Carthaginian's fielded a force of 10,000 heavy infantry (hoplites), which comprised citizen troops in the form of the 2500-strong Carthaginian Sacred band, but which was predominantly Libyan in makeup. A little under a century later, in 255 BC during the First Punic War, the mercenary general Xanthippus commanded on Carthage's behalf, to use Polybius' word, a 'phalanx'. Hannibal at the Battle of Zama in 202 BC commanded, again according to Polybius, a 'phalanx'. Now the obvious conclusion and one that has been drawn

51 A *kopis*, as shown on the Amazon frieze from the Mausoleum at Halikarnassos

52 Hoplite warfare, from a relief in the British Museum

## Units, Nationalities and Equipment

in the past, is that at the Battle of Crimisus, Carthage fielded hoplites and then, following the military trend of the period, had re-equipped by the First Punic War and fielded Macedonian-style phalangites. It has, however, also been argued that no such thing occurred, that Macedonian-style equipment was not adopted and that Carthage's close-order infantry remained armed with the spear as their primary weapons. Before attempting to answer these questions the first thing we need to do is describe exactly, in terms of equipment, what we are talking about.

Hoplite equipment, and in this context we are really talking about close-order spearmen, consisted of a long thrusting spear (of the type already described) and a large shield (52). The classic hoplite shield was round, approximately 1m in diameter. It was carried on the left arm and due to its weight which derived from a thin metal covering over a thick wooden core, it was stepped at the rim thus allowing the shoulder to help bear its weight in battle. Potentially crucially for the argument in favour of the Carthaginians' use of this style of equipment, such shields appear on the Simitthus-Chemtou monument (53). Alongside them, on the same monument, we also see Celtic-style oval shields, which can equally be used by close-order spearmen (54 & 55). The monument in question, which has been dated to the mid-second century BC, can be used to argue for a continuity in equipment style from the Battle of the Crimisus River to Zama.

The Macedonian phalangite also employed a round shield, although somewhat smaller and lighter than that carried by the hoplite (56 & 57). One example found

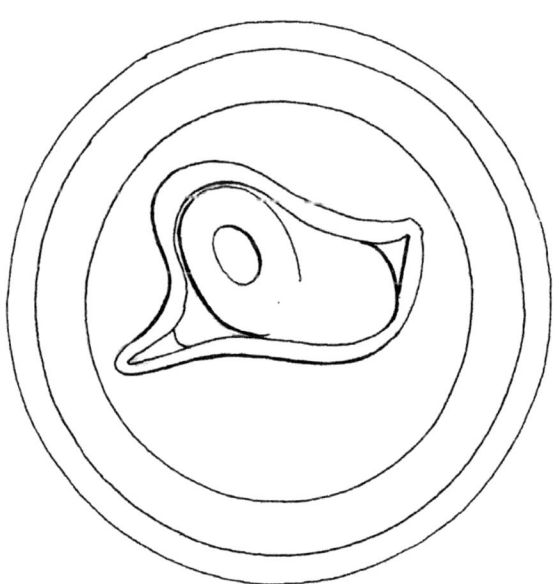

53 A hoplite style shield from the Simitthus-Chemtou monument

*Hannibal's Army*

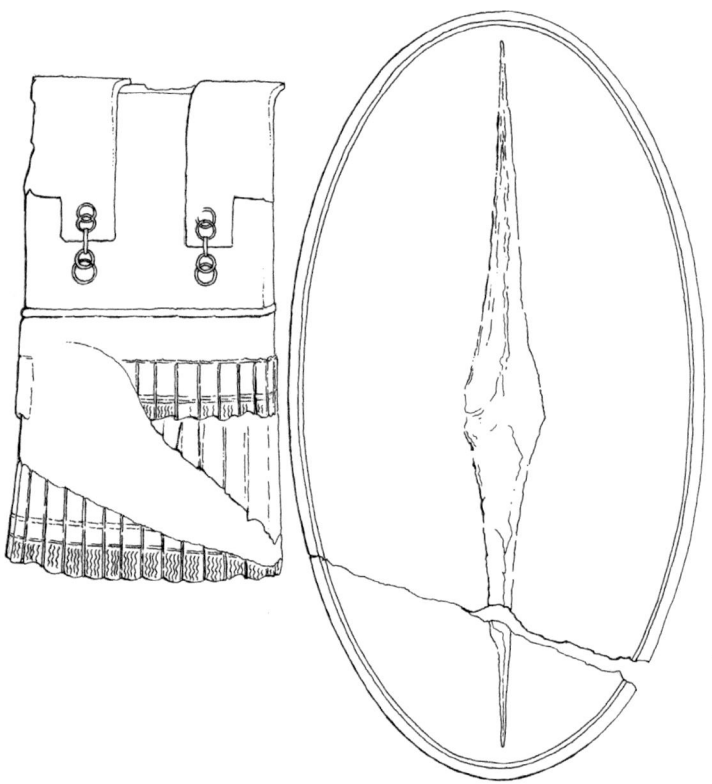

54 A mail or linen cuirass and Celtic-style shield from the Simitthus-Chemtou monument

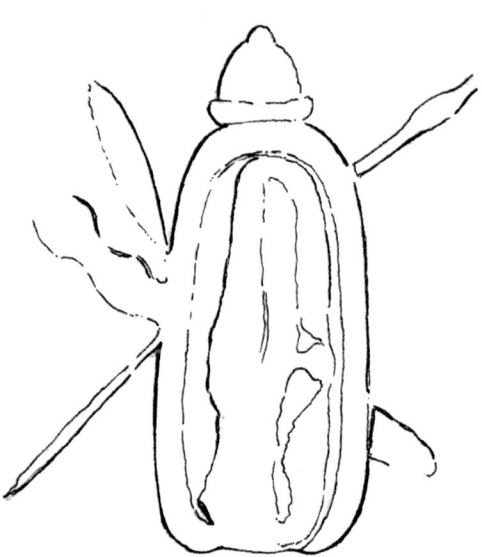

55 A warrior's panoply – Celtic style oval shield, conical helmet, sword, and spears – on a fragmentary Punic tombstone from D'El-Hofra à Constantine

*Units, Nationalities and Equipment*

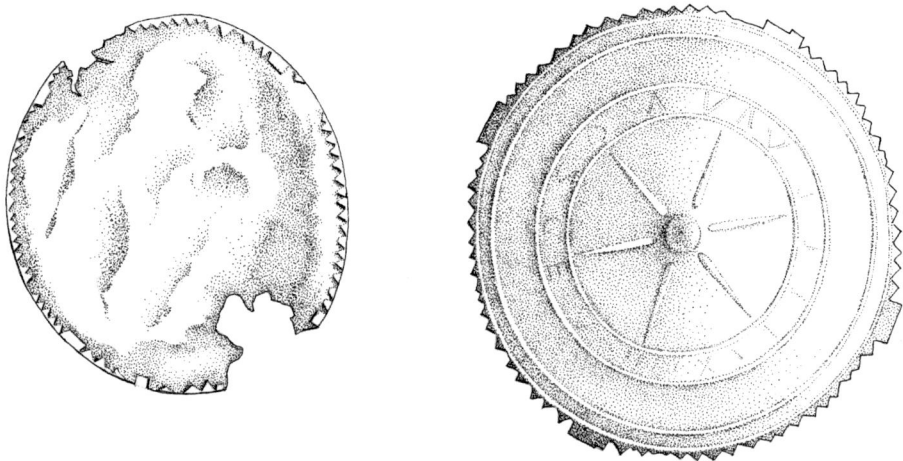

56   Macedonian phalangite shields. The plain example on the left is from Pergamon, the right-hand shield with the Sun blazon of Macedon is in the J. Paul Getty Museum, Malibu. *Drawn by M. Daniels after Connolly 2000*

57   A reconstruction of a phalangite's shield

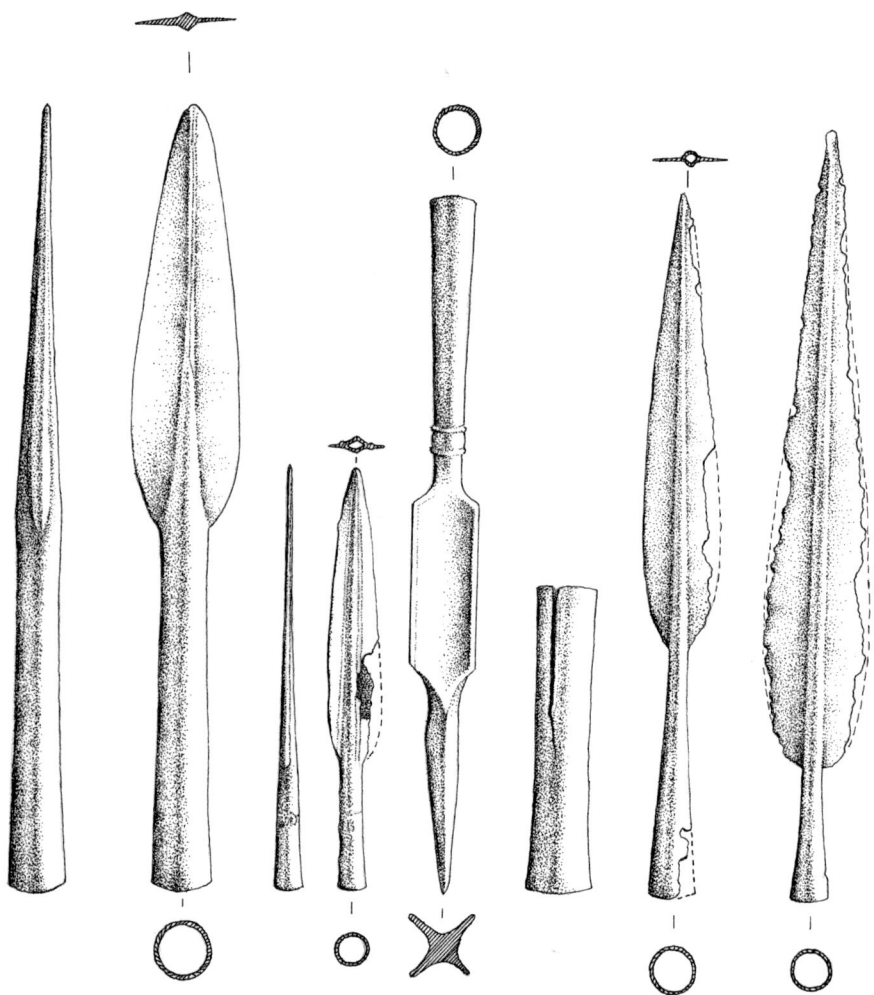

*58 The sarissa and associated finds from Vergina. Drawn by M. Daniels after Connolly 2000*

at Pergamon had a diameter of 63cm, while a similar find now in the J. Paul Getty Museum measures between 79.8-81.4cm in diameter. Again carried on the left arm, it was fitted with a shoulder strap to help bear the weight and in the process free up both hands, allowing the phalangite to wield his primary weapon – the *sarissa* (*58; colour plate 15*). The *sarissa* was to all intents and purposes a pike, the length of which has been much debated by modern authors. Theophrastus, writing in the fourth century BC, gives the length of the *sarissa* as 12 cubits, while Polybius in the second century BC states that in his day the length of the weapon was 14 cubits. In modern terms these measurements translate as 18ft and

*Units, Nationalities and Equipment*

59 Reconstructions of the Vergina finds

21ft respectively, based upon a standard Attic cubit. In length terms these tally perfectly well will Early Modern period pikes.

Finds from Vergina in Northern Greece (Macedonia) show that the *sarissa* was fitted with a large, heavy (it weighed 1.07kg) butt-spike to help counterbalance the weight and length of the shaft (*59*). The shaft itself, like later Renaissance and Early Modern pikes, then tapered to a small head (*60* & *61*). The far larger spearheads from the same find context may possibly be from a cavalry *sarissa*. The cavalry *sarissa* is usually depicted as having a proper spearhead at each end of the shaft and is also believed to have had a hand-grip, which may possibly explain the

60 The *sarissa*

61 Reconstructions of Early Modern period pikes. The small heads and tapering shafts of this weapon formed the basis for the latest reconstruction of the *sarissa* in 59 & 60

*62  The pike in action. The weapon is comparable in length to the sarissa in 60*

metal tube associated with the Vergina finds. The tube which is usually described in the context of the infantry version of the weapon as a 'coupling link' is both unique and unparalleled. It is believed to have been used so as to allow the weapon to be carried in two pieces – yet in battle this would have been an obvious weak spot allowing, if not extremely tight and well fitting, the weapon to literally fall apart. In the wear and tear of everyday use such an obvious design flaw seems unlikely and both the use of this find and its perceived universality in *sarissa* construction needs rethinking.

The *sarissa* was, as the Romans discovered, a truly formidable weapon (*62; colour plate 16*). Yet did the Libyans use it? In order to attempt to answer that question we need to look at the Carthaginian army in a broader context – namely that of the Hoplite and Macedonian military revolutions – and that is precisely what we shall do in the next chapter.

# 5

# Hellenisation

> As soon as the attack began Aemilius, advancing to the first ranks, found that the foremost of the Macedonians had stuck the heads of their pikes into the shields of the Romans, so that it was impossible for his men to reach their adversaries with their swords. And when he saw the rest of the Macedonians take their shields from their shoulders, join them close together, and with one motion present their pikes against his legions, the strength of such a rampart, and the formidable appearance of such a front, struck him with terror and amazement. He never, indeed, saw a more dreadful spectacle, and he often mentioned afterwards the impression it made upon him.
>
> Plutarch, *Aemilius Paulus*, 19

In many ways the answers to some of the questions concerning the Hellenisation or otherwise of the Carthaginian army lie not so much in the evidence for the Punic Wars, but rather in the Macedonian Revolution and the clash of the Roman legion and the Macedonian phalanx at Cynoscephalae, Pydna and Atrax. Yet in order to understand the answers we need to go back to the very beginning and the Hoplite Revolution. Prior to hoplite warfare we had what we today term the 'Homeric' battlefield, where despite the large numbers involved very few people actually engaged in close combat – the vast majority of the combatants were there to take part in the occasional missile engagement and to provide moral support to and an audience for the 'heroes' displaying their martial prowess. Raiding, rather than battle, constituted the main military activity.

The series of events we term the Hoplite Revolution or the creation of the 'Western Way of War' took place not in a matter of years, nor in the space of a few decades, but rather the process spanned centuries. Equally the whole process of creating close-order infantry combat occurred not simply on a physical, spatial level, it also had an ideological and psychological impact. Indeed at times the rationale behind and the mythology of hoplite warfare were as important as the panoply of weapons and the physical space surrounding an individual hoplite in the phalanx. The Hoplite Revolution was not simply technological, although the panoply was of decided importance, but stands rather as part of a more general shift in military tactics, for alongside it we see the hoplite becoming solely concerned with hand-to-hand combat, the segregation of troop types and the regimentation of formations. At the same time we see a philosophical underpinning as articulated in the literature of the period and an ideological triumph in the victories and defeats of the Persian Wars, where the Greeks successfully fought off the invasion of numerically superior Persian armies between 490 and 479 BC.

Having said that the creation of hoplite warfare was not simply technological, it was in a way technologically driven, in that the first stage of this revolution in warfare was the creation or appearance of the panoply or armour and everything else that followed derives from this (including the Macedonian revolution). Finds of a hoplite-style bronze helmet and a plate bronze cuirass from Argos have been dated to c.720 BC. Greaves also appear around this time. The distinctive hoplite shield itself came into use by around 700 BC. The traditional arms of the hoplite – thrusting spear and sword – were already in existence. Thus we see within the space of a generation at the end of eighth century BC the creation of all of the elements of the full hoplite panoply. It must be noted, however, that the minimum requirements for close-order infantry combat are nothing more than thrusting spear, shield and sword, and the universal adoption of this minimum only really occurred following the Persian Wars, with the rise of regimentation and the separation of troop types.

We begin in the seventh-century BC literature to see the articulation of the hoplite ethos and the mantras which over the century we have come to associate with close-order infantry combat. If the Argos finds mark, in archaeological terms, the beginning of close-order infantry combat, then the writings of the poet Tyrtaeus constitute the ideological foundation texts. Thus in the elegiac poems of Tyrtaeus we gain a picture of heads protected by helmets, of rounded shields advancing upon one another and of that most important of weapons 'man-slaying ashen spears'. Alongside these snapshots, these vignettes, of combat Tyrtaeus also and more importantly presents us with the honourable underpinning of, and the correct way of undertaking, this form of combat.

> Fear ye not a multitude of men, nor flinch, but let every man hold his shield straight towards the van, making Life his enemy and the black Spirits of Death dear as the rays of the sun … Those who abiding shoulder to shoulder go with a will into the mellay and the van, of these are fewer slain … For pleasant it is in

dreadful warfare to pierce the midriff of a flying man, and disgraced is the dead that lieth in the dust with a spear-point in his back ... let each man close the foe, and with his own long spear, or else with his sword, wound and take an enemy, and setting foot beside foot, resting shield against shield, crest beside crest, helm beside helm, fight his man breast to breast with sword or long spear in hand.

Tyrtaeus *Elegiac Poems*, 11

These words of Tyrtaeus, in one form or another, have echoed down the centuries. We see them in the *Moralia* of Plutarch, in Aristophanes comedy *The Babylonians*, in Thucydides, Polybius, Diodorus and beyond. The next step in the Hoplite Revolution was physical, whilst the one after that was ideological.

The end of the Archaic period, around 500 BC, saw a change in the depictions of combat on vase paintings and this is all probability reflected a real change on the battlefield itself. Thus we see a disappearance from the painter's repertoire, and from the ranks involved in hoplite warfare, of mounted hoplites, of javelins and Boeotian shielded figures, while archers go from kneeling and shooting amidst the ranks of hoplites to standing at the rear with unstrung bows. Now this is not to say that light and mounted soldiers were no longer used in Greek warfare – rather we are witnessing the beginning of the segregation of troop types and the creation of the classical phalanx. Despite Herodotus' mythologising, it is equally clear from his writing that this process was not fully completed until after the Persian Wars.

Marathon, the great Greek victory in 490 BC over the Persian invaders and the first major battle of the Persian Wars, even by the time Herodotus came to describe the battle, had been mythologised into an ideal. It had become a model hoplite attack, and yet even though in reality this was not the case, the thought of it, the idea of it as such is, and was, more important than the truth, for the psychological ripples of the battle are still felt today. Marathon stands as one of the foundation stones of the 'Western Way of War' precisely because of the power of the hoplite myth of the battle. The battle not only came to represent a physical triumph, particularly for the Athenians, it was also more importantly seen as an ideological triumph, demonstrating the superiority of civilised close-order hoplite infantry over the other, namely barbarian methods and forces. The dead of Thermopylae, and the victories of Plataea and Salamis, merely served to reinforce the lessons of Marathon and the Greeks' belief in *their* system of warfare. The fact that Salamis was a naval battle is neither here nor their, and affects the argument not one jot. For like its land-based equivalents, it showed once again that closing with and killing the enemy won battles – centuries later Nelson echoed the lessons of the Persian War in that his favourite signal was No.16: 'Engage the enemy more closely.'

The years leading up to and those of the Peloponnesian War saw the final pieces of the classical phalanx, the ultimate fruits of the Hoplite Revolution, fall into place. Popular misconceptions to one side, the Peloponnesian War of 431-404 BC was not noted for any major pitched battle. However, when such confrontations did occur, most notably at Delium in 424 BC and at Mantinea in 418 BC, then we see rank and file – close-order heavy infantry – in ordered seriated ranks whose primary weapon was the thrusting spear. This was the final stage in the development of the hoplite, but not of hoplite warfare for alongside the hoplite becoming a (single) spear and shield wielding heavy-infantryman who fought in a block completely separate from his lighter armed and mounted compatriots, we see the beginning of the rise of distinct units of light infantry and cavalry. The hoplite remained the 'queen of the battlefield', but they now formed only part of an increasing range of tactical options, built on a variety of specialties. Delium in 424 BC has been dubbed as heralding the birth of tactics, for as well as deployment of usual depth on the Boeotian right wing (here the Theban's were massed 25 deep) we also see the (victorious) Boeotians successfully co-ordinating bodies of infantry and cavalry in order to crush the Athenian infantry and thus win the battle. Alongside an increasing role for cavalry, both on and off the battlefield, the Peloponnesian War and subsequent fourth-century conflicts saw an increase in the numbers and importance of peltasts, javelin-armed light infantry. Such trends are mentioned specifically by Xenophon in his account of the Persian Expedition, and such troops could, given the right set of circumstances, even defeat hoplites, as the Spartans discovered to their cost at Sphacteria in 425 BC when they were beaten by the Athenians. Peltasts were, of course, not the only specialist light infantry employed by the Greeks, for we also see slingers and archers fighting alongside blocks of hoplites. Finally, according to the historian Diodorus the first artillery pieces, tension machines to be precise, were created in 399 BC by Greek engineers working for Dionysius I, tyrant of Syracuse. All of the pieces were now in place for the Macedonian Revolution, although as will be seen, one of the most important components of that revolution – the *sarissa*-armed phalanx - had been attempted before. The Hoplite Revolution, although certainly more profound, appears very slow, when compared to the Macedonian Revolution.

In the 370s BC the Athenian general, Iphicrates, attempted military reform. He failed, but some 15 years later Philip II, King of Macedon, succeeded in creating a military revolution. Why did one succeed where the other failed and was the latter aware of the former's failure? According to the later authors Diodorus Siculus (15.44.2-4) and Cornelius Nepos (*Iphicrates* I.3-4), and both use near identical words, Iphicrates:

... changed the arms of the infantry. While before he became commander they used very large shields, short spears and little swords, he on the contrary exchanged peltae, or Thracian shields for the round ones (for which reason the infantry have since been called peltasts), in order that the soldiers might move and charge more easily when less burdened. He doubled the length of the spear and increased that of the swords; he changed the character of their breastplates, giving them linen in place of bronze cuirasses or mail. In that way he made the soldiers more active; for while he diminished the weight of the armour, he contrived to protect their bodies equally well without overloading them.

Cornelius Nepos, *Iphicrates* I.3-4

Neither Nepos, nor Diodorus, writing in the first century BC, appear to have appreciated that a fourth century BC Greek peltast was the equivalent of a Roman *velite*. However, given that the *velite* appears to have disappeared from use, as a specific type of legionary, in the second century BC (they last appear in Sallust's account of the Jugurthine War, 46.7) this mistake seems less surprising. Leaving this error to one side and turning to the rest of the text we see that in effect Iphicrates was attempting to create what we have come to know as a phalangite. Light armour and smaller lighter shields provided an acceptable degree of protection, although less than that provided by the hoplite panoply, but any difficulties were meant to be offset by the greater manoeuvrability (decades later Philip was able to feign retreat of his phalanx at the Battle of Chaeronea) and the greater reach of the double length (16ft approx.) spears. Such a weapon equivalent in length to the Macedonian *sarissa* and the far later Byzantine *menavlion*, would, like its successors, have had to have been used two-handed and would equally potentially have had a great deal of stopping and penetrating power. Iphicrates' experiment, however, failed, the potential of the new spear went unrealised and Athens continued to arm its hoplites in the traditional classical manner.

Where Iphicrates failed Philip II succeeded – the reasons in part being captivity and autocracy. Between 368 and 365 BC Philip was a hostage in Thebes. Well treated and under the influence of Epaminondas, the greatest general and statesman of the day, he was able to gain what amounted to an insider's insight into Theban military supremacy. Thebes was at this point ascendant – why? Well as Philip will have not failed to notice and as Hammond states, the secret (which is not really all that secret):

lay in constant 'training, practice, experience and action', the development of an elite infantry unit (The Sacred Band), the use of shock tactics, and the co-ordination of infantry and cavalry in battle.

Hammond, 1994, 10

As well as observing the Thebans at first hand, Philip was also in a position to absorb the lessons and developments of the last century or so of Greek history. As for Iphicrates, that was less than a decade in the past and given the 'inventor's' esteemed reputation it is more than likely that these events were known to Philip.

Autocracy allows a certain freedom. It allowed Philip to create his own model army. It allowed him to use the yield of the Pangaeum mines (1000 talents per annum, from the gold and silver mines) and the new economic growth of Macedon (which was partly a result of conquest and partly a result of alliance) to keep his forces in the field all year round and here we see a crucial factor, one which not only ensured Macedonian success, but which set the pattern for all subsequent successful armies (states) – namely professionalism.

The cardinal elements of Philip's new force were an infantry cavalry combination – but one like no other. The infantry follows Iphicrates' model, and was absolutely first rate – it needed to be if Philip was to compete with the states of southern Greece and achieve his dream of domination. With the cavalry arm, Macedon, like Thessaly, had an existing tradition upon which to build. However, as with the infantry, he went beyond what had been seen before and created a body of *sarissa* armed, highly drilled, mounted shock troops. Of course having the ability to create and indeed creating a so-called 'Ever-Victorious Army' are not enough. Other factors came into play and Philip possessed them. Philip has been largely eclipsed by his more famous son, yet the army Alexander uses to such great effect was the product of Philip's successful imitation of its Theban progenitor. Success breeds success, victories breed victories, experience is cumulative, and not only amongst the men but also amongst the officers, in that a corps of marshals was also created. Thus Philip was able to lead the Macedonian army to victory against a variety of enemies in the Balkans, Illyria, Thrace, Macedonia itself and Greece, with the crushing of the allied Greeks at Chaeronea in 338 BC being his best remembered victory. Philip's victories were achieved because of battlefield asymmetry. The asymmetry sprang from the weapon system itself, for both infantry and cavalry were *sarissa* armed and both fought at close quarters with the enemy. In terms of equipment the phalangite, although equipped with a sword was primarily armed with a *sarissa*, which as we have seen was a 12-14 cubit-long pike (Theophrastus and Polybius respectively, 18-21ft), allowing Philip, as earlier with Iphicrates, to reduce the burden of armour. Although he was still protected by helmet, greaves, cuirass and shield, the phalangite was more manoeuvrable and thus more flexible than the hoplite. Equally with the points of the first five ranks of the phalanx projecting in front of the formation, these Macedonian pike blocks presented not simply a devastating killing machine but a near impenetrable infantry frontage. Philip's new shock cavalry, the Companions, were, like the infantry, well equipped and protected by metal helmets and cuirasses in order to allow them to engage in hand-to-hand combat – they killed with *sarissa* and sword. Complementing these cardinal elements were light infantry – hypaspists, peltasts, slingers, archers and light cavalry units, as well as a siege and engineering train incorporating the latest in torsion-powered artillery. The primary weapon itself – the *sarissa* – although extremely simple in conception and design, since it was basically a long spear, required a great deal of training (or drill) in order to work properly – this Philip provided, not just in the normal campaign season but all year round. This new level of professionalism, and we see a rise in professionalism stemming from the Peloponnesian War and exemplified in Xenophon's account of the Persian expedition, coupled with the weapons, the well-balanced combination of unit types and the aggressive nature of Philip's system, which took the 'Western Way of War' to new heights, created the asymmetry between his forces and those of his opponents. Successive victories only served to compound and deepen this imbalance and explain the Macedonian conquest of the Persian Empire.

On the death of Philip in 336 BC, his son Alexander inherited a superb instrument in the Macedonian army and it was an instrument which he knew how to wield. For if there was one thing that he, Alexander, was good at it was killing. The asymmetry becomes more pronounced in Alexander's Persian campaigns, where numerical supremacy was as naught compared to the qualitative superiority of the Macedonian army and its commander. Thus with the exception of the Granicus River, where the forces were roughly equal, in all of his other major engagements – Issus, Gaugamela and at the Hydaspes River – Alexander, constantly and comprehensively defeated forces which were at least twice his size. The scale of Alexander's conquests stands out, but they fit within the general scheme and pattern of Western warfare, and thus we see similar victories (against numerically superior enemies) for example by Caesar at Alesia and the British at Rorke's Drift.

Alexander died in 323 BC, much we suspect to the relief of his generals. His death ushers a new age of Western warfare, one beset by problems and one which ended in the 160s BC with the Romanisation of the surviving Hellenistic armies, and it is in this age that we must place the Carthaginian army and ask how Hellenic was it? Did it follow the model of the Successor States or did it follow a different path? However, before we answer those questions we need to look at the armies of Alexander's heirs and at the wars of the Romans against them, as well as the reasons behind the Romanisation of these armies. For in answering these questions we can begin to answer the questions surrounding, and thus go some way to understanding, the Carthaginian Army.

The problems faced by the 'Western Way of War' in the Hellenistic period and which occurred during the time of the Successor States stemmed from the rise, or the return, however one wishes to see it, of symmetry between opposing forces. Symmetry occurs, of course,

> Where arm and equipment on both sides were approximately the same, and they normally were in encounters between the principal powers.
>
> Van Creveld 1991, 97

On his death Alexander left behind a vast empire. However the problem was not the size of the Empire, but its newness. Lacking a long-standing system of government and control as well as a credible heir, Alexander's senior generals immediately set to squabbling. Some of their number were promptly disposed of, while the rest, the survivors, proceeded to divide the territory between themselves. Out of this initial power struggle five kingdoms emerged – those of Ptolemy, Seleucus, Antigonus, Antipater and Lysimachus. The stage was now set for the Wars of the Successor States, in which various attempts were made to reconstitute, to a greater or lesser extent, the kingship and Empire of Alexander. More, bigger and heavier sums up the warfare of this period. All the advantages enjoyed by Philip and Alexander were now to all intents and purposes gone. The reason is quite simple, for as well as dividing up the territory and creating spheres of control they also, in order to protect their newly-formed kingdoms, they divided up the armed forces. Thus when the inevitable conflicts broke out it was very much a case of like versus like.

The wars of the *Diadochi*, the Successors, stand out as a period marked by tactical success and strategic failure. The Battle of Ipsus in 301 BC of course stands out, in that it saw the death of Antigonus and the destruction of his kingdom; this result was against the general trend, yet in terms of the forces involved it was very much a product of its time.

The immense wealth of the Persian Empire, and for that matter the others states plundered by Alexander, fuelled the warfare of the period and such riches were needed. For gone was loyalty to the *polis*, gone too was Macedonian nationalism. Armies were highly professional, they campaigned all year round, but equally they employed vast numbers of mercenaries, on a scale never before seen. These mercenaries required (as indeed did the non-mercenaries) constant financial remuneration for services rendered.

At the Granicus River in 334 BC and at Issus in 333 BC the Macedonian army numbered some 19,000 men, while at Gaugamela 331 BC it numbered a mere 22-23,000 men. Within a generation following the death of Alexander battlefield numbers had reached astronomical levels. At Ipsus in 301 BC there were at least 80,000 men on each side, with Hanson (1989) suggesting that there may have been as many as a quarter of a million on the field. This vast increase in numbers from the days of Philip and Alexander was both a result of the new economic and political forces at play and an attempt on the part of various Successors to break the stalemate and achieve hegemony.

Alongside manpower solutions we also see technological and esoteric attempts to overcome the problem of symmetry. The most obvious and straightforward weapons system change was the lengthening of the *sarissa*. In Polybius' day it was 21ft long, yet he tells us that it was longer in the past (XVIII.29). Thus given that Theophrastus was writing in the fourth century BC and Polybius in the second century BC we can place the latter's long 16 cubit or 24ft *sarissa* in the third century BC, the period of the Wars of the Successors. Probably widely copied, yet given its subsequent shortening, not entirely successful, the 16 cubit *sarissa*, although possibly allowing a sixth row of spear points to project forward, was in all probability too unwieldy to be used properly.

> ... the monster elephants plunged this way and that among the lines of infantry, dealing destruction in the solid mass of the Macedonian phalanx.
>
> Arrian *Life of Alexander the Great*, V

Elephants become a feature of western warfare following Alexander's conquests of Persia and India and, along with *cataphracts* and scythed chariots, were the new terror weapons of the age.

Some works on ancient warfare, particularly children's books, portray the war-elephant as the tank of the ancient world. Yet this analogy only works (to some extent) if one compares elephants to the 1916 British Mark I tank – in that, like the Mark I, it was erratic in its movements, did not always go in the intended direction, was susceptible to enemy fire and was more frightening in appearance than in force of arms.

Porus' elephants in the fourth century bore simply a mahout (or handler) and a warrior. This picture rapidly changed and, as was detailed in the previous chapter, by the early third century Pyrrhus' elephants carried crenellated towers which, dependent upon the size of the elephant, could carry up to four men, while by the second century BC we see the Seleucids employing fully armoured elephants in battle. Alongside an increase in the beast's load we also, obviously, see an increase in the number of elephants deployed on the field of battle. Thus the 15 elephants which Darius failed to use at the Battle of Gaugamela were nothing compared to the 475 elephants deployed at Ipsus, while at Raphia nearly a century later in 217 BC we see nearly 200 elephants engaged. Elephants, despite

## Hannibal's Army

their erratic nature, could and were used successfully most notably by the allies at Ipsus, but also by the Romans at Cynoscephalae and Magnesia. Equally the fact that the Romans twice imposed the condition in the Treaty of Apamea (189 BC) which required the destruction of the Seleucid elephants corps, along with the fact that tactical manoeuvres (Zama 202 BC), traps (Megalopolis 318 BC) and contraptions (Gaza 312 BC) were all employed, alongside field artillery, to counter the threat of elephants in battle, shows that they were considered a real threat. However, their erratic nature undoubtedly counted against them and despite the Emperor Claudius' use of them during his first century AD invasion of Britain, in the West war elephants were very much a product of, and confined to, the Hellenistic period.

From Livy's description of them at the Battle of Magnesia (Livy XXXVII.41) and Xenophon's description in the *Hellenica* (IV.I.17), scythed chariots were purely and simply a terror weapon, at their most effective against inexperienced or dispersed troops. More controllable than elephants they were nevertheless more vulnerable, being easily disabled by steady experienced troops, and thus they had very limited currency and were not widely adopted.

The *cataphract*, basically a heavily armoured man on an armoured horse, stands as the most successful and enduring of the Hellenistic attempts to break the deadlock of symmetry, in that they continued to be used well into the medieval period. The origin of the *cataphract* lies on the steppes of Central Asia and in the armies of the Achaemenid Persians. Yet the *cataphract* itself was a product of the third century BC and the need to deal with the problem of symmetry as well as to provide a possible cavalry solution or counter to the phalanx. Whilst it is harder to reconstruct the appearance of *cataphracti* in the beginning, compared say to its apogee under the Imperial Roman and Sassanian Empires, it is possible thanks to a find of what is believed to be a complete set of *cataphract* armour (which includes lamellar and scale elements) from the Hellensitic city of Ai-Khanoum in Afghanistan. This find along, again, with Livy's description of Magnesia and the Pergamon reliefs, point to the fact that Ammianus' description of such cavalrymen as 'statues polished by the hand of Praxiteles' was pertinent not only to his own day, the fourth century AD, but was equally apposite and applicable to the third and second centuries BC (Ammianus Marcellinus, XVI.10.8). In this description of iron statues seemingly come to life we see the shock, awe and terror such troops were intended to excite in the enemy. The armour, however, also served another purpose. The *cataphract's* primary weapon was the *contus,* which was basically a form of *sarissa*. The weapon, the *contus/sarissa*, due to its reach, gave the *cataphract* the ability, in theory, to engage close-order infantry formations. What changed the theory to practice was the high level of armour worn by man and horse. This new, unprecedented level of protection increased confidence at both a personal and a unit level, promoted boldness and as a consequence allowed the *cataphracti* to not only close with and engage, but to attempt to crack open the enemy's heavy infantry formations.

> The glitter of arms strikes very great fear in the enemy.
> Vegetius, *Epitome Rei Militaris*, II.14

Scythed chariots, elephants and *cataphracti* all worked primarily on the principle enunciated by Vegetius and this was true no matter whether they were facing horse or foot.

Little has been said so far of light-troops, of slingers, archers and peltasts, or for that matter of siege warfare. Sieges do not really stand as a feature of the Carthaginians in the Second Punic War, with all of the main episodes – Marcellus' great and successful siege of Syracuse and Scipio's escalade of New Carthage – being conducted by the Romans. That is not to say that the Carthaginians did not participate in this activity, rather we are concerned with the Carthaginian army on the field of battle. However, before we return to our primary subject we must continue with our contextualisation. Light troops, slingers, archers and javelin-throwers who fought the little war between the lines before the main bodies clashed, were employed by all of the armies of the day. Yet despite earlier successes in the Peloponnesian War and later under the likes of Iphicrates, and despite their usefulness in raiding and ravaging, their use on the battlefields of the Hellenistic period was decidedly limited. For example in the *Anabasis* of Xenophon (V.4.22-4) we see Greek archers and peltasts standing and engaging the enemy, who incidentally flee upon the arrival of the hoplites. However, in this case the enemy were barbarians, Mossynoici to be precise, one of the many tribes the 10,000 Greek mercenaries encountered on their march home from the centre of the Persian Empire, in 401-400 BC. Such a feat was not really possible in the Hellenistic period. In the wars of the Successor States they had a role to play, but that role was diminished due to their fragility. Missile troops (in effect light infantry) were fragile because they were unable to sustain a heavy enough rate of 'fire' to prevent them being overthrown by a determined force of infantry or cavalry armed with hand-held close combat weapons, thus their diminished success. They were of course still used in their traditional roles, as well as in the new role of both attacking and protecting elephants (as for example occurs at Paraetacene in 317 BC). However, the symmetry of the period counted against the effective co-ordination of arms leading to the issue being decided by the efforts of the close-order troops of both infantry and cavalry.

Where then into all of this does the Carthaginian army fit? How Hellenistic was it? How was it equipped? What exactly was meant by Polybius (III.114.1) when he stated that:

> The Africans were armoured in the Roman fashion, Hannibal having equipped them with the choicest of arms captured in the previous battle.

Before, however, we can answer these questions we need to look to the campaigns of Pyrrhus, the Battles of Cynoscephalae, Magnesia, and Pydna and the siege of Atrax, at legion versus phalanx and at the Romanisation or reform of Hellenistic infantry in the 160s BC. Our view of the Roman world and the Roman way of war is very much conditioned by the simple fact that they won. Equally our image of the Roman army is one of the Imperial Army – the army of Trajan's Column and the first and second centuries AD. Yet the certainties of the Imperial Period were not be so obvious in the third and second centuries BC and it was by no means clear which child of the Hoplite revolution, either the Roman or Macedonian, would prosper; indeed at the time it may well have seemed that the latter had the more promising future.

We view the triumph of Roman arms, particularly in the wars against Macedon and Antiochus, as a triumph of flexibility. Of the flexibility of the mind, made physical in the manipular system. It was yet another triumph of the 'West' as an ideal and as such a further promotion of our belief that Rome, not Macedon nor the Successor States for that matter, stood as the true descendant of Greece. However, in the century or more between the war against Pyrrhus in the early third century BC and the Romanisation of the Ptolemaic and Seleuicid armies in the mid-second century BC, matters were not, as indeed Lendon (2005) correctly argues, so clear cut.

Polybius in his history (XVIII.29) reviews the reasons for the success and failure of the phalanx. Polybius was of course possessed of the advantage of hindsight. While for those Romans who had faced the phalanx in battle the issues were readily apparent and not so clear cut. Aemilius Paulus even went so far as to describe the Macedonian pike phalanx as the most terrifying thing he had ever seen (Polybius, XXXIX.17). By 280 BC the Romans had most definitely abandoned their Servian hoplite system in favour of the maniple (sub-units). Yet in a series of three engagements at Heraclea (280 BC), Asculum Satrianum (278 BC) and Beneventum in (275 BC) all against Pyrrhus' phalangites, they singularly failed to demonstrate the supremacy of their new system. True the Romans won the final battle, but the middle engagement was indecisive, while the first was a definite Roman defeat.

Leaving aside for one moment the battles of the First and Second Punic Wars the next real test of legion versus phalanx came at the siege of Atrax in 198 BC and in the hills of Cynoscephalae in 197 BC during the Second Macedonian War. According to Livy (XXXII.17) the Romans besieging Atrax, which was in Thessaly, believed that once a breach had been achieved then the city would undoubtedly fall. However, things did not go as planned. The Macedonian garrison formed their phalanx in the gap, and the Romans failed to make any headway against them. As a consequence, and with winter coming on, the Romans were forced to abandon the siege.

After the indecisive nature of the conflict against Pyrrhus, the siege of Atrax stands as a decided triumph for the phalanx. Cynoscephalea, like its far later and indeed more famous parallel Gettysburg, began as an encounter battle. Encounter battles, such as Cynoscephalae and Gettysburg, are messy affairs, in which both sides upon contact do not withdraw, rather they pour in more troops as they appear, whether or not they are ready. In such circumstances command and control is weak. Chance and circumstance thus play a far greater role than do the commanding generals preconceived plans or orders of battle. Cynoscephalea, as a battle, embodied the best of both systems. The Macedonian right wing charging down hill proved unassailable and legion gave way to the phalanx. Flaminius, the Roman commander, starring defeat in the face, took charge of the Roman right wing and placing his elephants to the front, led the attack against the enemy's left which had just marched into position and had not as yet deployed for battle. Flaminius was therefore able to utterly rout and pursue the Macedonian left. Thus each side had gained success on their own right and experienced failure on the left. The issue was decided by a tribune on the Romans' successful right flank, who upon seeing that he was now above and more importantly to the rear of the Macedonian right, detached and led a force of some 20 maniples against the victorious Macedonians. Taken by surprise, and assailed from both fronts and rear, the Macedonian right disintegrated. The battle was an undoubted Roman victory. However the initial success of the Macedonian phalanx, coupled with the fortuitous battle-winning initiative displayed by the Roman tribune mainly served to demonstrate the strength of the different systems.

The next great clash of legion and phalanx came at the Battle of Magnesia in 190 BC, during Rome's war against the Seleucid King Antiochus III. There are a number of reasons for the Roman victory at Magnesia, although the primary faults revolve around Antiochus himself, in that he failed to adequately co-ordinate his polygenous force and that he committed the cardinal sin of overpursuing, thus failing to support his phalanx in its hour of need. As for the phalanx itself, Livy (XXXVII.42) and Appian (*Syrian Wars* 35) tell us that adjacent friendly contingents sought shelter within and thus disrupted the phalangites' formation and it was only after this occurred that the legions attacked. Appian (*Syrian Wars* 35) provided the most detailed description of the destruction of the Seleucid phalanx.

The Roman missile storm forced the phalanx back and that caused it to disintegrate. Magnesia, like Cynoscephalae, was a Roman triumph, yet the failure to close with and the method embarked on to disrupt even an already disrupted phalanx shows how formidable such a formation was. The most frightening thing Aemilius Paulus ever witnessed was the Battle of Pydna in 168 BC. The battle, which brought to an end the Third Macedonian War, marked the end of an era, in that it was the last of the great contests between the legion and the phalanx. Pydna was a short, sharp nasty battle which lasted less than an hour and one which opened well for the Macedonian phalanx. Deployed on level terrain with secure flanks, the Romans were unable to make any headway against the hedge of *sarissa* points presented by the Macedonians – quite the contrary in fact. For not only did the points of the *sarissa* stick into Roman shields and prevent them from closing to contact, but the sheer pressure exerted by the phalanx forced the legions back (Plutarch, *Aemilius Paulus*, 19.2). The Macedonian phalanx's initial success was, however, ultimately its downfall. The Romans retreated without breaking onto rough terrain which causes natural gaps and tears to appear in the phalanx. These were exploited by the Romans to dreadful effect, finally able to use their swords against the enemy, and the Romans entering via these gaps literally hacked the phalanx apart from the inside.

Pydna effectively ended Macedonia as an independent sovereign state, it also, in what Lendon calls 'The Wrath of Pydna' (2005, *Soldiers & Ghosts*, 193) settled the legion versus phalanx debate once and for all, for after this event we see the Romanisation of Hellenistic heavy infantry. It is a truism that successful armies are copied, albeit usually in the most superficial of terms, and that is precisely what happened in the years following the conclusion of the Third Macedonian War. The Hellenistic period, as we view the passage of time, may not have been over but the Hellenistic military revolution was. The Seleucid and Ptolemaic armies proceeded to Romanise their close-order heavy infantry. Gone was the *sarissa*-armed phalanx; in its place we see the heavy infantry of the Hellenistic kingdoms organised and equipped entirely along Roman lines. Despite the views of some later commentators, there was no inevitability about the change, in crude terms the legion proved more successful than the phalanx and in terms of a score card for the above engagements we see that the Roman legions won four battles (Beneventum, Cynoscephalae, Magnesia and Pydna) while the phalanx prevailed in only two of the seven battles (Heraclea and Atrax) and the engagement at Asculum Satrianum was indecisive – these figures, however, mask the problems the Romans faced in overthrowing the Hellenistic phalanx. Yet in the end decisions are at the time made more on the basis of perception than analysis and this is what we see here – the last battle (Pydna) viewed in the light of a century or more of a simple win/lose breakdown would obviously put the Roman system ahead and promote change. Indeed a similar process occurred after the Franco-Prussian War – the Prussian Army was copied around the world based upon the fact that it had won the war. The reality was that the glory of French arms was eclipsed not because they were poorly equipped, trained or lacking in martial spirit, quite the contrary, rather they were poorly led and out-generalled by Von Moltke. To this theme of successful armies being copied we will return in due course. Where then into all of this does the Carthaginian army fit?

In their fourth-century wars in Sicily and North Africa against Timoleon and Agathocles, the Tyrant of Syracuse, we see in the pages of Diodorus and Plutarch the Carthaginians fielding a hoplite army. Yet this army was one shaped by the events of the Peloponnesian War, for alongside citizen infantry and the elite Sacred Band, we see mercenaries, cavalry, Balearic slingers and even chariots.

Going on to the First Punic War in 264 BC the question of Hellenisation raises its head. Greek influence in the Carthaginian state has already been discussed and indeed the hoplite army of the fourth century provided no better example of this influence. However, the question of how pervasive this influence was is hard to answer. Rome, Carthage's great and ultimately triumphant enemy, although not immune to Greek influence, plotted its own course, albeit one built on the firm foundations of hoplite close-order infantry warfare. Did Carthage follow a similar path? Certainly it had far greater connections with the Greek world. These came primarily as a result of trade and, as we have seen with the case of Xanthippus, that trade included the hiring of mercenaries at quite a senior level of command or military expertise, however we choose to define it. Equally their wars in Sicily against Timoleon and, more importantly in Hellenistic terms, Pyrrhus, brought them into direct contact with the military mainstream of the Greek and Hellenistic kingdoms. Countering this pull was their westward horizon, particularly Spain. Thus, as with Rome, Carthage was both a part of and apart from the prevailing military orthodoxy.

Of course the main question concerns the *sarissa*. Did the Carthaginians, specifically Hannibal, field units of *sarissa*-armed infantry and if so did he after his earlier victories and before Cannae re-equip them with captured Roman equipment? Given the importance of this we will deal with it last and turn instead to hopefully more straightforward matters. The problem, as articulated in *Interpretatio Romana*, even with the straightforward, is the lack of information. Certain points do stand out, thanks to the surviving literary evidence – Pyrrhus, Xanthippus and the Barcids in Spain. Other aspects, particularly the semantics of the word mercenary in a Hannibalic context, are, as Griffith noted, merely concerned with the 'splitting of hairs' (1935, 231).

The Carthaginians' encounter with Pyrrhus, viewed by many as the greatest general of his day, in Sicily in the 270s BC was probably the catalyst for the introduction of elephants into Carthage's military repertoire. The question of the influence of Pyrrhus' Macedonian-style phalanx in harder to answer.

Carthage's next brush with the mainstream of Hellenistic military thinking came during the First Punic War with the hiring of the Greek mercenary general Xanthippus. His appearance, at the height of the crisis precipitated by Regulus' invasion of North Africa, saved Carthage. Xanthippus' expertise and success derived from his Spartan training, his ability to speak the same technical language as the mercenaries employed by Carthage, his drilling of Carthaginian army in the Spartan manner and his demonstration of the correct use of Carthage's strength in terms of elephants and cavalry (Polybius I.32.1-8). Regulus' defeat and capture in 255 BC effectively ended the Roman invasion of North Africa and also any hope for an early end to the war. However, although the Xanthippus incident, along with other aspects of the First Punic War, allows us to glimpse the Carthaginian army, details in the main elude us. Elephants and mercenaries are a commonplace of Hellenistic warfare and Carthage's use of them is not surprising. Equally the various contingents, allied, tributary and mercenary, who formed the Carthaginian army are again not unusual – indeed purely national armies were a thing of the past. However, with Carthage, except in times of crisis such as the Mercenary and Third Punic War, the citizen contingent was reduced to command and control; generals and their staff. The wealth of the city was used to hire troops to take the place formerly filled by the citizens themselves.

Although we are able, in the case of the First Punic and Mercenary War, to sketch a picture of an army which is broadly Hellenistic, we fall down when we turn to the question of how were the heavy infantry – the Greeks and Libyans – equipped? For despite Polybius (I.33.6? I.34.6) twice referring to the 'Carthaginian phalanx' we lack a sense of the equipment of this 'phalanx' – sadly the word is too generally used in this instance to attach a specific meaning. There is even a studied vagueness about Polybius' use of the word Carthaginian in this context. It is usually taken to mean a force of Carthaginian citizens. However, it appears at times (I.33 & I.34) to refer to the whole army and at other times to the non-mercenary portion of the army, which could be a citizen force (perhaps the city was in danger) but could also include Libyan infantry. The problem with the word phalanx is that it simply means a body of infantry in close formation and it was used to describe Greek hoplites, Macedonian phalangites (with whom the term is most commonly associated) as well as the Roman legion. We thus need more information than simply the word, to say what exactly it means in a particular context and in the case of the Carthaginian army we lack the evidence to give a definite meaning, although as will be seen we can make an educated guess.

Failure in the First Punic War and Roman perfidy during the Mercenary War led to the expulsion from Sicily and the loss of Sardinia, as a result Carthage turned to Spain. Spain allowed the Barcids, Hannibal being the most famous scion of that particular family, to dominate Carthaginian politics. Politically Spain restored Carthage's imperial pride and its national wealth. Militarily it provided a springboard from which to launch an invasion of Italy, it also provided men, particularly heavy infantry armies of the type that today would be considered Roman, yet at the time was instead indigenous to Spain and in point of fact provided a model which Rome copied (certainly in terms of sword type, probably in terms of one of the precursors to the fully developed *pilum*).

Finally the *sarissa* or spear? How Hellenistic was Hannibal's Army? Opinion is of course divided. To take but two moderate views, Goldsworthy in *The Punic Wars* (2000, 55) stated that:

> Neither the Roman nor the Carthaginian possessed a modern army based on the Hellenistic model, but the campaigns between them were to be fought largely in the manner of contemporary Hellenistic warfare.

Lendon, however, in his *Soldiers and Ghosts: A History of Battle in Classical Antiquity* (2005, 204) believed that:

> The Romans had been fighting the Macedonian phalanx for more than a century. Pyrrhus defeated the Romans with it in the early third century, the Carthaginians in Africa in the middle of the century did as well, and Hannibal did the same later.

Who is correct? Of course as with most things Punic and particularly the Carthaginian army we lack the evidence for a definitive answer, thus the divergence of opinion, we must therefore weigh what we do have and make a decision based upon the balance of probability – in some ways the Carthaginian army was Hellenistic, in others it was not. Possibly not the most satisfactory of answers, but Carthage, like Rome, to some extent went its own way although unlike its great adversary, was more influenced by the Greek and Hellenistic world than was Rome.

Greek and Hellenistic ideas and fashion were absorbed via conflict in Sicily and North Africa against Timoleon, Agathocles and Pyrrhus, as well as via the hiring of Greek mercenaries to fight for and lead Carthaginian armies, as well as from the likes of Silenos and Sosylos who formed part of Hannibal's personal entourage. Thus we see the Carthaginians forming polygenous armies: fielding mercenaries and elephants with towers, employing missile troops whilst recognising their fragility, conducting siege operations yet recognising the primacy of the pitched battles. Equally the Carthaginians, like the Athenians, took a hard line against generals who were perceived to have failed, while after Cannae we see Hannibal acting like a model of a Hellenistic general and expecting a Roman surrender (after three such defeats it would have seemed obvious to any normal state that they were beaten – Rome was not a normal state and in this Hannibal had fatally misread his opponent). However, with some of the more esoteric elements – such as *cataphracti* and scythed chariots – it is obvious that Carthage did not field a state-of-the-art, modern Hellenistic army.

In terms of equipment we are fairly well informed about many of the various contingents who made up the Carthaginian and particularly Hannibal's army. Where we fall down is over the equipment of the Libyan (and by extension in time of crisis the Carthaginian citizen) heavy-infantry, although the real debate concerns their primary weapon. In terms of body-armour, helmets, greaves and swords we would expect to see, for both officers and men, a range of equipment – Hellenistic-style helmets as well as iron, bronze, and linen cuirasses, alongside what we tend to view as more Italian/Roman style patterns. What we probably would not see is the *sarissa*. It may have been used in the First Punic War, then again it may not; the language of the available written evidence is too vague to reach any meaningful conclusion. Whatever the case, it seems that this weapon was not carried by Hannibal's army during his invasion of Italy, nor from our evidence does it appear to have been used by any other Carthaginian force during the Second Punic War.

Descriptions of what we, today describe as legion versus phalanx encounters (such as Pydna and Cynoscephalae) contain an element of shock and awe and of the irresistible power of the phalanx. This is lacking from the descriptions of the battles of the Second Punic War – none of the Roman commanders in Spain, Italy or North Africa suffered, so far as our evidence allows, from an Aemilius Paulus moment. Rather we see what appear to be similarly equipped armies engaged, the outcome relying upon factors other than the primary armament of the close-order heavy infantry. In particular and practical terms the shields of the Simitthus-Chemtou reliefs, which in all probability reflected contemporary Libyan military equipment, cannot be used with a *sarissa*. Finally, and most damningly we come to Hannibal re-equipping his troops with the spoils of Trasimene. Successful armies are copied, unsuccessful ones are not, it is a platitude, but it is none the less correct. Polybius (3.87.3) tells us that after the Battle of Lake Trasimene Hannibal

> ... rearmed the Africans in Roman fashion with select weapons, being, as he now was in possession of a very large number of captured arms.

Trasimene was Hannibal's second greatest victory, and his second successive victory in as many years. Thus as far as he was concerned everything was working, his army was a winning army. All the years of campaigning in Spain were paying off. In these circumstances changing not only the equipment, but also the tactics and fighting style (for that is what we are talking about) of the Africans does not make sense – particularly as the legionary was fundamentally a swordsman, whereas the phalangites most definitely were not. Equally changing a winning system for a system which has twice lost is, I believe without precedence. Such a change would have impacted badly upon the morale of the African/Libyan thus re-equipped, for they would have been expected to fight in a new way without, it would appear from our sources, any attempt at retraining. Flodden in AD 1513 stands as a prime example of an army's failure to properly adopt a new weapon system, and even here we see the normal practice of copying the most successful weapons system of the day. Polybius (3.87.3) only really makes sense if the Libyan/African was already equipped and fought in a manner similar to their legionary counterparts, and what we are seeing, after Trasimene, is Hannibal simply taking advantage of a stock of better quality, albeit similar, equipment. We are not seeing a major change in fighting style, merely a qualitative and quantitative increase in particularly the armour, but also the weapon of the close-order, Libyan heavy infantry.

The Carthaginian army, Hannibal's Army, then was to a large extent Hellenistic, particularly in respect of organisation and outlook, but also to some extent in terms of equipment. Indeed in those respects, more so than the Roman Army, it was not fully Hellenistic, as gaps and omissions in its troop types and equipment set it apart from the mainstream. Its reputation today in the main rests upon the ability of its most famous general who welded the various elements together. However, in the face of a well led, well trained and highly effective Roman army, the Carthaginian army, along with its city and empire, was ultimately defeated.

# Select Bibliography

The following bibliography lists the main, and at times the most accessible secondary works, used in researching this subject. It is thus not comprehensive. However, these secondary sources themselves contain bibliographies, which spread the net, so to speak.

Adcock, F.E., *The Greek and Macedonian Art of War* (Berkeley, 1957)
Addison P. & Calder, A. (eds), *Time to Kill: the soldier's experience of war in the West 1939-1945* (London, 1997)
Ashley, J.R., *The Macedonian Empire* (Jefferson, 2004)
Bar-Kochva, B., *The Seleucid Army: organisation and tactics in the great campaigns* (Cambridge, 1976)
Bar-Kochva, B., *Judas Maccabaeus: the Jewish struggle against the Seleucids* (Cambridge, 1989)
Bath, T., *Hannibal's Campaigns* (Cambridge, 1981)
Bishop, M.C. & Coulston, J.C.N., *Roman Military Equipment* (2nd ed., Oxford, 2006)
Carlyle, T., *On Heroes, Hero-Worship and the Heroic in History* (London, 1840)
Chaniotis, A., *War in the Hellenistic World* (Oxford, 2005)
Churchill, Winston S., *The Second World War*, Vol. IV: The Hinge of Fate (London, 1951)
Connolly, P., *Hannibal and the Enemies of Rome* (London, 1978)
Connolly, P., *Greece and Rome at War* (London, 1981)
Daly, G., *Cannae: the experience of battle in the Second Punic War* (London, 2002)
Feugèure, M., *Casques Antiques* (Paris, 1994)
Foley, R.T., *German Strategy and the Path to Verdun: Erich von Falkenhayn and the development of attrition, 1870-1916* (Cambridge, 2005)
Gaebel, R.E., *Cavalry Operations in the Ancient Greek World* (Norman, 2002)

Goldsworthy, A., *The Punic Wars* (London, 2000)
Goldsworthy, A., *Cannae* (London, 2001)
Griffith, G.T., *The Mercenaries of the Hellenistic World* (Cambridge, 1935)
Hammond, N., *Philip of Macedon* (London, 1994)
Hanson, V.D., *The Western Way of War: infantry battle in Classical Greece* (Oxford, 1989)
Hanson, V.D., *Why the West has won: carnage and culture from Salamis to Vietnam* (London, 2001)
Head, D., *Armies of the Macedonian and Punic Wars 359BC-146BC* (1982)
Healy, M., *Cannae 216BC* (Oxford, 1994)
Hoffmeyer, A.B. de, *Arms and Armour in Spain: a short survey* (Madrid, 1972)
Howarth, D., *Waterloo: a Guide to the Battlefield* (London, 1980)
Hoyos, D., *Hannibal's Dynasty: Power and politics in the western Mediterranean 247-183BC* (London, 2003)
Keppie, L., *The Making of the Roman army: from Republic to Empire* (London, 1984)
Lancel, S., *Carthage: a history* (Oxford, 1995)
Lazenby, J.F., *Hannibal's War* (Warminster, 1978)
Lazenby, J.F., *The First Punic War* (London, 1996)
Lendon, J.E., *Soldiers & Ghosts: a history of battle in classical antiquity* (New Haven, 2005)
McCall, J.B., *The Cavalry of the Roman Republic* (London, 2002)
Moreno, P. (translated by D. Stanton), *Apelles: the Alexander mosaic* (Milan, 2001)
Peddie, J., *Hannibal's War* (Stroud, 1997)
Pleiner, R., *The Celtic Sword* (Oxford, 1993)
Polito, E., *Fulgentibus Armis* (Rome, 1998)
Ritchie, W.F. & Ritchie, J.N.G., *Celtic Warriors* (Aylesbury, 1995)
Scullard, H.H., *The Elephant in the Greek and Roman World* (London, 1974)
Sekunda, N., *Republican Roman Army 200-104BC* (Oxford, 1996)
Sekunda, N., *Hellenistic Infantry Reform in the 160s BC* (Lodz, 2001)
Snodgrass, A.M., *Arms & Armor of the Greeks* (Baltimore, 1999)
Stead, I.M., *British Iron Age Swords and Scabbards* (London, 2006)
Stephenson, I.P., *Romano-Byzantine Infantry Equipment* (Stroud, 2006)
Stephenson, I.P. & Dixon, K.R., *Roman Cavalry Equipment* (Stroud, 2003)
Tarn, W.W., *Hellenistic Military & Naval Developments* (Cambridge, 1930)
Van Creveld, M., *Technology and War* (Oxford, 1991)
Van Wees, H., *Greek Warfare: myths and realities* (London, 2004)
Warmington, B.H., *Carthage* (London, 1960)
Wise, T., *Armies of the Carthaginian Wars 265-146BC* (London, 1982)
Yalichev, S., *Mercenaries of the Ancient World* (London, 1997)

# INDEX

Achaemenid Persians  106
Agathocles, the Tyrant of Syracuse  34, 111, 113
Alexander (the Great) of Macedon  17, 39, 47, 102-105
Al-Sumaa weapons grave  52, 73
Aemilius Paulus  30, 58, 97, 108, 110
Ammianus Marcellinus  13, 106
Antigonus  104
Antiochus III  17, 109
Aristophanes  99
Appian  29, 44-45, 73, 109
armour:
    Greaves  61, 83, 85, 98
    helmets  51, 58, 61, 67, 69, 72, 74, 76, 78-79, 98
    iron cuirass  83
    linen cuirass  67-69, 83
    mail  56, 67, 69
    muscled cuirass  69, 82, 98
    *pectoral*  63, 69, 82
    shield  52, 55-56, 63-64, 67, 69, 73-74, 85, 89-92, 98, 110
    under-armour padding  58, 69
Arrian  47, 73
Asclepiodotus  42-43
Athens  14, 100
Aztecs  22

battles (and sieges):
    Adrianople  18
    Adys  26
    Aegatos/Aegates Island  15, 27
    Alamein  15
    Alesia  103
    Asculum Satrianum  108, 110
    Atrax  97, 108-110
    Beneventum  108, 110
    Cannae  15-18, 20, 25, 28-29, 31, 33-34, 37, 39, 67, 69
    Caudine Forks  15, 18
    Chaeronea  101-102
    Crimisus River  87, 89
    Cynoscephalae  97, 106, 108-110, 114
    Delium  100
    Desert Storm  18
    Ecnomus  26
    Flodden  115
    Gaugamela  103-105
    Gettysburg  108
    Granicus River  104
    Great Plains  29
    Heraclea  48, 108
    Hydaspes River  47, 103
    Ipsus  104-105
    Issus  103-105
    Magnesia  42, 106, 108-110

Mantinea  100
Marathon  33, 99
New Carthage  107
Paraetacene  107
Platea  99
Pydna  97, 108, 110-111, 114
Raphia  42, 105
Rorke's Drift  103
Saguntum  45
Salamis  99
Somme  25
Sphacteria  100
Syracuse  16, 107
Telamon  51, 53, 72
Teutonberg Wald  18, 23
Thermopylae  99
Trasimene  17, 25, 28, 33-34, 37, 114-115
Trebia  17, 25, 28, 33-34, 37
Waterloo  35
Zama  16, 20, 29, 34-35, 37, 39, 41, 43-44, 87, 89, 106
Bosch  25
Bramocar  31

Carthaginian army (national contingents):
  Balearic Islanders  19, 39-40, 43, 52, 111
  Carthaginians  23, 35, 41, 72-94, 112-115
  Celts/Gauls  19, 23, 39-40, 45, 51-61
  Greeks  19, 39
  Italians  39, 67-72
  Libyans/Africans  19, 35, 39, 72-94, 112, 114-115
  Ligurians  19, 39, 45, 51, 53-61
  Numidians/Mauri  19, 23, 30, 39, 41, 45, 72-94

Spanish/Iberians  19, 23, 39-40, 45, 61-67
*cataphracti*  106-107, 114
Cato the Elder  25, 30
Cold War  25-26
command and control  31-33, 41-42
Cornelius Nepos  17, 101

Dante  25
*De Rebus Bellicis*  58
Diocletian  38
Diodorus  45, 55-56, 61, 101, 111
Dionysius I  100
Domitius Ahenobarbus  58
Dürer, Albrecht  22

Ebro river  28
elephants  19, 34, 42-43, 47-50
Epaminondas  101

Flaminius  109

Gisgo  31
Glanum  55
Gundestrup Cauldron  55

Hamilcar Barca  27-28, 30-31, 49
Hannibal (son of Hamilcar Barca)  16-18, 23, 25, 28-29, 31, 33-35, 37, 39, 42, 49, 67, 72-73, 87, 111, 113-115
Hanno son of Bomilcar  31
Hasdrubal  31
Hasdrubal (son of Hamilcar Barca)  31, 34
Hasdrubal (son-in-law of Hamilcar Barca)  28, 31, 42
Henry VIII, of England  21
Herodotus  99
hoplite  87, 89, 97, 101, 112

Incas  22
Iphicrates  100-102

Julius Caesar  17, 49, 73

*Kabinettskrieg*  13
Kitchener, Field Marshal  16

Lee, Robert E.  17, 33
Livy  22, 32, 44-45, 49-50, 55, 66-67, 73, 106, 109
L. Manilus Vulso  26
Lyson and Kallikles, tomb of  78, 83

Macedonian army  39, 43, 97, 104, 109
Mago  31-32
Maharbal  31, 33
Marcellus  38, 50
M. Atilius Regulus  26-27, 32, 34, 112
Marlborough, 1st Duke of  13, 47
Massinisa  45, 49
Mercenaries  19, 35, 43-45, 112
Military equipment  46-95
Muttines  32
Myrcan  31

Napoleon I  17, 33
Nelson, Horatio  99
*Notitia Dignitatum*  56
Numantia  69

Orange, arch at  55-56

Peloponnesian War  14-15, 43, 100, 103, 111
Pergamon frieze  87
Persian Wars  98-99, 103
Phalangite  47, 89, 102, 112
Philip II of Macedon  20, 83, 100-103, 105

Philip V of Macedon  31
Plutarch *Moralia*  99
Polybius  16, 18, 23, 38, 40, 49-50, 55, 60-61, 64, 67, 87, 92, 99, 102, 105, 108, 112
Porus  47
Ptolemaic army  18, 49, 110
P. Cornelius Scipio Africanus  16-17, 29-30, 34-35, 38-39, 107
P. Cornelius Scipio Aemilianus  30
Pyrrhus  25, 48-49, 105, 108, 111-113

Q. Fulvius Nobilior  49

Revolutionary and Napoleonic Wars  15

saddle  53-55
Schwartzkof, Norman  17
Scythed-chariots  105, 114
Seleucid army  18, 42, 47, 49, 109-110
Silenos  23, 114
Simitthus-Chemtou monument  83, 89, 114
skirmishers  50-52
Sosylos  23, 114
Spanish Civil War  26
Sparta  14-15, 23, 41, 100
Strabo  52

Tacitus  22
Tanks  105
Theophrastus  92, 102, 105
Timoleon  81, 111, 113
Trajan's Column  46, 52, 56, 73
Tyrtaeus  98-99

unit size  39-41

Vachères warrior  58
Vegetius  107

Virgil  73
Von Clausewitz  13, 26
Von Moltke  33-34, 111

War of the Spanish Succession  13
War of the Successors  104-105
weapons:
   artillery  100
   bow  50, 99, 107
   *Contus*  106
   dagger  52
   *Falarica*  66-67
   *Falcata/Kopis*  52, 63, 85
   javelin  50-51, 64, 73, 99
   *Menavlion*  101
   pike  93

*Pilum*  72, 113
*Sarissa*  47, 92-95, 102, 105, 107, 110-111, 113-114
sling  50, 52
*Soliferreum*  66
spear  50-52, 60, 67, 69, 76, 85, 98, 113
sword  60-61, 63-64, 69, 73, 76, 85, 98, 113
Wellington, first Duke of  25, 35, 46

Xanthippus  26-27, 32-33, 39, 41, 87, 111-112
Xenophon  100, 106-107

Zonaras  48

# Also available from The History Press

The Late Anglo-Saxon Army

I.P. Stephenson

978 0 7524 3141 3

As a result of the Battle of Hastings the late Anglo-Saxon army has had a bad press, more famous for its defeats than its victories. In this study the author looks at the history, organisation, tactics and equipment of the army and argues that rather than being a failure, the late Anglo-Saxon army was not only adaptive, but also innovative, and doesn't deserve its rather dubious reputation.

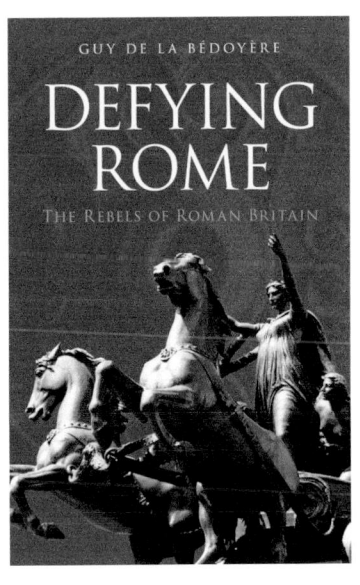

Defying Rome
The Rebels of Roman Britain

Guy de la Bédoyère

978 0 7524 4440 6

Rome's power was under constant challenge and nowhere moreso than in Britain. From the beginning to the end of Roman rule in Britain a succession of idealists and chancers, most famously Boudica, tried to expel Rome and recover their lost power. This book covers 14 rebellions and explains why Britain was such a hot-bed of dissent.

For further information please go to: www.thehistorypress.co.uk

# Also available from The History Press

Chester AD 400-1066
From Roman Fortress to English Town

David Mason

978 0 7524 4100 9

This is the most up-to-date general account of Chester from the late Roman period to the Norman Conquest. Its author tells the story of Chester; its disappearance into obscurity during the 'Dark Ages', its emergence as an important religious, commercial and military settlement in the Kingdom of Mercia and the everyday life of its people leading up to the advent of Norman rule.

Roman Dorset

Bill Putnam

978 0 7524 4104 7

At the time of the Roman invasion present-day Dorset was part of the territory of the Durotriges. The Second Legion Augusta was responsible for the conquest of this area and Bill Putnam charts the remarkable extent to which Roman ideas, life and language were adopted in the years following this conquest. This book is the result of 40 years of fieldwork and research by the author.

For further information please go to: www.thehistorypress.co.uk

# Also available from The History Press

The Anglo-Saxon Kingdom of Lindsey

Kevin Leahy

978 0 7524 4111 5

Lindsey was a small Anglo-Saxon kingdom that lay to the south of the Humber Estuary. Over the last 50 years, this kingdom has emerged from its own 'dark age' to reappear as a highly prosperous and sophisticated area that was on the edge of great events with a flourishing Christian culture until the Viking invasion of AD 877.

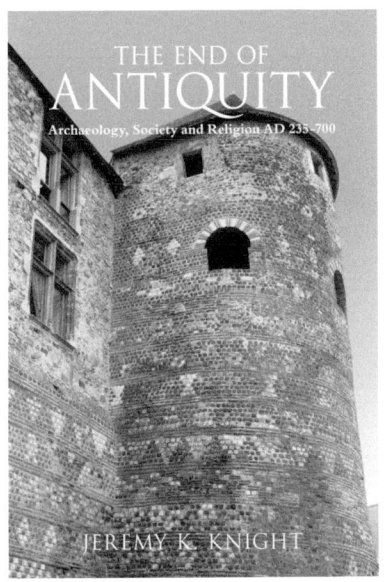

The End of Antiquity
Archaeology, Society and Religion AD 235-700

Jeremy K. Knight

978 0 7524 4082 8

This is a masterful study of the transition from the Classical world to Medieval Europe and has won widespread critical acclaim.

'For this well written, well illsutrated and scholarly book, he has placed all students of Late Antiquity in his debt' - *Antiquaries Journal*

For further information please go to: www.thehistorypress.co.uk

# Also available from The History Press

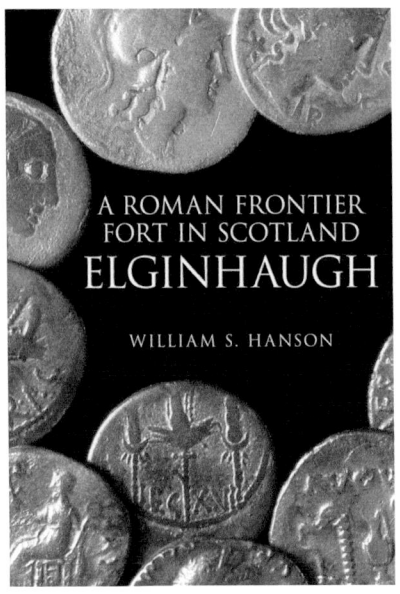

A Roman Frontier Fort in Scotland
Elginhaugh

William S. Hanson

978 0 7524 4113 9

Elginhaugh is the only completely excavated timber-built auxiliary fort in the Roman Empire. Here the excavator, Prof. W.S. Hanson tells the story of its discovery and excavation, interprets the evidence and discusses the nature of military life on the furthest northern frontier of the Empire in the first century AD and its impact on the local area.

Britannia Prima
Britain's Last Roman Province

Roger White

978 0 7524 1967 1

This important work counters the widely held view that when the legions left Britain the Roman way of life disappeared with them. In fact Britannia Prima – broadly the west of Britain – had from the fourth to the sixth centuries a distinctive Romano-British character and successfully resisted significant Anglo-Saxon invasion longer than any other area of Britain.

For further information please go to: WWW.THEHISTORYPRESS.CO.UK

# Also available from The History Press

Winchester
From Prehistory to Present

Tom Beaumont James

978 0 7524 3742 2

The story of Winchester is both chequered and colourful. Tom Beaumont James takes the reader on a fascinating journey through the history of this great city, from its beginnings as a pre-Roman tribal centre, through its roles as Anglo-Saxon capital and its decimation by the Black Death, to its dramatic revival in the age of steam.

Concepts of Arthur

Tom Green
978 0 7524 4461 1

Ever since the 12th century there has been an effort to show that the Arthur of Celtic legend was based on an historical figure. In this re-examination of all the early literature Tom Green argues that far from being an historical figure mythicized, Arthur emerges as a mythical and/or folkloric figure historicized. Looking at the latest research into Celtic and Indo-European deities, the author concludes with the suggestion that Arthur may well have been a local deity, the product of a pre-Christian mythology.

For further information please go to: www.thehistorypress.co.uk